GW01605204

A FRIEND FROM THE WOODS

A FRIEND FROM THE WOODS

by

E. M. WATKINS

VICTORY PRESS
LONDON and EASTBOURNE

Reprinted 1976
ISBN 0 85476 185 3

Printed in Great Britain for
VICTORY PRESS (Evangelical Publishers Ltd.),
Lottbridge Drove, Eastbourne, Sussex,
by Fletcher & Son Ltd, Norwich

CONTENTS

CHAPTER ONE

BEN'S BIRTHDAY

When Ben first awoke he did not remember that it was his birthday. All that registered was that it was Saturday, he didn't have to get up early, eat breakfast in a hurry, or catch the school bus. Saturday mornings had a nice leisurely feeling about them, although at the week-ends Ben was expected to do more about the farm.

He yawned and flexed his knees, watching the bumps they made in the patchwork bedcover. Through the window the sky was a soft, clear blue with scarcely a cloud in sight—a real spring day. The starlings under the eaves outside Ben's room were quarrelling and screeching noisily. They had nested there for so many years that he scarcely noticed them any more. Then realisation came to Ben that today was no ordinary Saturday—it was his twelfth birthday and perhaps this year . . .

He threw back the bedclothes and sprang from his bed with a bound, pulling on his jeans and old grey sweater which were on the floor where he had left them. There was water in the jug on the old-fashioned washstand, and he dipped in a sponge and rubbed his face with it. His morning ablutions completed, Ben bounded noisily down the stairs and into the kitchen, full of hope. The younger children were all there, waiting for their breakfasts. At sight of him the twins, Rachel and Anna, looked at each other and giggled coyly. Ben ignored them and went through into the adjoining dairy. His mother was turning the handle of the milk separator, a job which on a Saturday usually fell to Ben.

He was fond of the dim, cool dairy and lingered for a moment in the doorway, watching his mother at work. Mrs. Laura Jackson was a strong, energetic woman with dark hair which already had a few streaks of grey in it. She wore a flowered wrap-around overall over her old tweed skirt, and the sleeves of her jumper were rolled above her elbows, showing her muscular forearms. Ben's father said she was as strong as a man. The separator whirred and chugged as it gained speed, its bell tinkling loudly at every turn. Ben moved forward and his mother turned and saw him.

"Oh, Ben—finish this, will you?" she said, with a slight air of preoccupation. "I must get breakfast."

Ben took the handle. Birthday or no birthday, the jobs had to be done.

"Happy birthday," said his mother, rumpling his hair as she went into the kitchen. Ben grinned, his heart lifting. Perhaps this year he would get his heart's desire, the thing for which he had longed for what seemed all of his life.

He worked at the handle extra hard. The faster he turned the sooner the job would be over. Soon the bell's clear tinkle became muffled in tone, the signal that it was time to turn on the little tap beneath the bowl. Ben watched the frothy, white milk bubble out in a thick stream and disappear into the metal pipes. Presently the skimmed milk came gushing out of the larger pipe into the waiting bucket, and a little later a thin stream of yellow cream poured from the smaller pipe into the earthenware crock. When the crock was full it would be well stirred and set aside until it was sour, and eventually Ben's mother would turn it into butter.

Ben's stomach began to rumble with hunger, and, the separating finished, he washed his hands at the scullery tap and went into the kitchen. His father had come in and was sitting in his place at the head of the table. His brown face and hair were shining from being sluiced under the cold tap, and his eyes, the brightest blue Ben had ever seen, were twinkling as they did when things were going well.

"Happy birthday, son," he said and Ben hung his head, a little embarrassed at being the centre of attention.

It was the custom of the Jackson family that birthday presents be opened ceremoniously after breakfast. Ben suddenly wished that the custom could be changed. It was bad enough having everyone stare while he opened his presents, without first having to get through a meal with everyone's attention focused on him. Rachel nudged Anna; they looked at each other and dissolved into one of their sudden and helpless fits of giggles. He glowered at them both. Stevie, the baby of the family, leaned from his high chair and upset his plate of porridge into the lap of five-year-old Mary, who began to shriek.

In the resulting pandemonium Ben's birthday status was forgotten for a while, and he felt grateful to his small brother. During the diversion he was able to gulp down his own porridge and consume a large portion of bacon and egg. He was beginning on his third slice of toast when he realised that everyone else had finished and was waiting expectantly.

"Is that boy still eating?" exclaimed his mother, who had been to the scullery with a load of dirty dishes. "I declare I don't know where he puts it all."

"He's all right—just growing," said his father kindly.

"It's time for the presents," said Anna, shrill with excitement. She produced a small, weighty parcel from beneath her chair and handed it over importantly. It was a joint effort from herself and her twin, and proved to be a handsome pocket knife, complete with a tinopener, corkscrew, and a gadget for getting stones out of horses' hooves. Ben could remember having admired it in Harris's the ironmongers last time he was in town, and he felt a rush of warmth towards his sisters. He tested the edge of the blade against his thumb.

"Thanks," he said. "It's a super knife."

"We saved our pocket-money for weeks to get it," said Rachel with eight-year-old smugness.

Mary had recently learned to knit, and her offering was a garter-stitch scarf, rainbow-striped, and decidedly narrower in some places than others. Ben almost never wore a scarf, and would not have been seen dead in this one; nevertheless he wound it around his neck at once and the little girl glowed with pride. Stevie, at two-and-a-half, was excused from giving presents, so there was just his parents' to come. They looked at each other and he knew it was something special. Ben's heart almost stopped as his father got up and went through into the sitting-room. He knew, he just knew, that he would come back carrying a roly-poly little puppy—a spaniel or a terrier perhaps; or maybe the puppy would trot along behind.

When Mr. Jackson returned he was carrying a very large, lumpy, and mysterious-looking parcel in his arms. The little girls and Stevie squealed with excitement and curiosity, but for a moment Ben felt only numbness. There was no puppy, just as there had been no puppy all the other years. All his hopes and plans and dreams had once again been in vain.

His father placed the parcel beside Ben's chair.

"Open it, Ben—open it," urged the twins.

Ben came to his senses and thanked his parents and began undoing the string. When the wrappings were removed a brand new, green canvas tent, complete with pegs, ropes, and poles, came into view, together with a groundsheet and handsome, quilted sleeping-bag. Ben had wanted camping equipment for a long time, but had never hoped to get it. It must have cost his parents a considerable amount of sacrifice. He tried to make his voice enthusiastic as he thanked them again, but a small, aching voice was saying somewhere inside him, "It's not a dog—it's not a dog."

His mother and father seemed to sense that something was wrong.

"You'll be able to go camping now with Chris Martin," said his father as he put on his cap and jacket in preparation for going outdoors to his work.

"Yes—I will," muttered Ben.

His father went out by the back door and the younger children scattered to their various pursuits. Ben gathered up his presents and prepared to take them to his room. As he reached the door his mother stopped him.

"Ben, what is it?" she asked, her brown eyes troubled. "Something's the matter, isn't it?"

"No," muttered Ben, turning away his head.

"Aren't you pleased with the camping gear?" she persisted, laying her hand on his arm. "Daddy and I thought that was what you wanted. You were so keen on going camping with Chris last summer."

"I am pleased with it—I am," said Ben desperately.

How could he explain that no gift, however elaborate, could possibly compare with a dog—a friend—of his very own?

"You're still hankering after a dog, aren't you?" said his mother shrewdly. She sighed, and went on, "We've been into it all before, Ben. You know why we can't let you have a puppy."

Ben knew. He had heard all the arguments. They could not afford to feed another dog, let alone one that did not work. Toby, the elder of the two sheepdogs, was old and crotchety and fought any strange dog that came near the place. A puppy would lead a miserable life on the Jackson farm, his father had said. When Ben said that he could keep the puppy always with him and let it sleep in his room, his mother was horrified.

"I'm having no dogs sleeping indoors," she said firmly, and Ben knew she meant it. Even old Toby and Floss were not allowed to set foot inside the house. They trailed Ben's father to the back door and lay on the mat until he came out again. "And what would happen while you were in school?" his mother had continued. "I know how it would be—I'd have the creature under my feet and I'd be clearing up after it all day, with all I have to do already. No, I won't have it."

Ben could see the sense of these arguments. He knew that his father was having a hard struggle to make ends meet, especially since he had recently bought the farm from his former landlord. He knew that his mother was sadly overworked, though she seldom complained. Another dog was unnecessary, but still Ben longed and hoped that they would change their minds.

He shook off his mother's arm and turned towards the stairs.

"I just—I just want something for a friend—something of my own," he said in a low voice, trying to explain.

"But you have friends," said his mother, puzzled. "You have your school friends, and the girls, and Chris Martin—lots of friends. I just don't understand."

Ben began to climb the stairs, shoulders hunched. He hardly understood himself. He only knew that there was an emptiness somewhere inside him, an ache for something all his, that he could love and that would love him in return. His parents loved him and meant well, but he could never make them see.

"It's all right," he said in a muffled tone, and took the last few stairs at a run. In his room he put the camping gear carefully in a corner and laid the gay striped scarf in a drawer. He slipped the knife into his pocket, making sure that the pocket had no holes it could fall out of. He wandered over to the mirror above his dressing chest and critically considered his reflection. A thin, pale face sprinkled with freckles stared sadly back at him. Untidy brown hair in need of a cut, large blue eyes like his father's but not such a bright blue—more a grey-blue like a rainy sky. A lonely face, thought Ben, overcome by a surge of self-pity.

He heard the tractor start up outside and went to the window. His father had hitched up the new hydraulic harrows borrowed from Mr Martin, and was on his way to work down the ground in the Four Oak field, ready for spring corn. Ben's eye fell on the two sheepdogs, one black and white and one brindled, trotting behind the tractor, and the ache inside him became suddenly unbearable. He turned away from the window, flung himself down on the unmade bed and cried as though his heart would break.

CHAPTER TWO

SUNDAY AT THE JACKSONS'

But the hearts of twelve-year-old boys are not so easily broken. By the next morning Ben had put his disappointment behind him, although the nagging little empty feeling was still somewhere inside him.

Sunday at the Jackson farmhouse was quite different from other days. Some things were the same, of course: the animals and the poultry had still to be fed, and the milking had to be done; but apart from these necessary tasks, no work was done on Sunday. Instead, when breakfast was over, the children would change into their best clothes, Ben's mother would put the dinner into the oven to cook, and then they would all pile into the ancient Ford car and drive to the church they attended in Hadley, the nearest town.

Until the age of twelve the children did not attend morning service, but went instead to Sunday school. This would be Ben's first Sunday morning service in the church.

He did not really look forward to it. He supposed it would be much the same as the Sunday evening service, with hymns, prayers, and a rather boring sermon to sit through. Ben knew that his parents were different from most other people in that they attended church, read the Bible, and prayed. In fact, they were often something of an embarrassment to him because of these things. Some of the neighbours laughed at them, he knew. Once he had mentioned this to his father, and his father had opened the big Bible and showed him a verse which said, 'I am not ashamed of the gospel of Christ: for it is the power of God unto salvation to every one that believeth.'

"Your mother and I felt some years ago that we weren't living the sort of life that pleases God. So we asked God to forgive us because we realised that the Lord Jesus had died for us," said his father. "Since we did that, we have tried, by His help, to follow His commands, and that includes reading His Word—the Bible—praying to Him, and joining with other people in church to worship Him, no matter who laughs at us. We trust that one day you will feel the same as we do."

Ben wished that he had not brought up the subject. His father did not often 'preach' at him, but when he did it had a way of making him feel very uncomfortable. So from then on he said nothing, even when sneers came his way.

As Ben took his place in the church beside his parents that morning, his main feeling was one of hunger. Breakfast seemed a long, long way behind him and dinner an equally long way in the future. As the first hymn ended, Ben's stomach rumbled loudly, and he glanced around in embarrassment. But apparently no-one had heard, or if they had they were too well-mannered to show it. The service continued: prayers, another hymn, announcements, and at last the commencement of the sermon. Ben leaned back in the hard seat and hoped it would not be a long one.

He gazed at the familiar face of their minister, the Reverend Pearce, who had iron-grey hair and a nice smile. Mr. Pearce was short-sighted and had special spectacles which he put on every time he wished to consult his Bible or his notes. For want of something better to do, Ben began to count the number of times the glasses went on and off. He had got to six when he suddenly became aware of what the minister was saying.

"Have you ever felt disappointed and disillusioned; that life has cheated you in some way?" enquired the minister in his deep, clear voice. "Is there a feeling of loneliness in your heart, an empty place that nothing seems to fill?"

Ben stared at Mr. Pearce, wondering how he had guessed. That was exactly how he himself felt, especially when he thought of the dog he had longed for. He sat up straight and began to listen, completely forgetting about Mr. Pearce's spectacles.

"These feelings could be due to the fact that you haven't a right relationship with God," the minister went on. "All of us were born sinners, and we can't expect to have happiness and joy with sin in our hearts. God loved us so much that He sent His only Son, Jesus Christ, into the world to be punished for our sins, to die on a cross, that we need not be punished. But we must be willing to admit our sin, and ask God's forgiveness, before we can have the happiness and peace He offers us." He went on with his sermon, leaving Ben thinking hard. For the first time he realised that he really was a sinner, for was he not often greedy, selfish, ungrateful, and dozens of other bad things? Didn't he often make his parents look sad by something he said or did? His longing for a dog, for instance. They had explained reasonably why it wasn't possible, but still he would not accept their reasons. The more Ben thought about it the blacker his sins seemed. He could hardly wait until the sermon ended and the last hymn was sung. He tugged at his father's coat sleeve as the people began to file out.

"Dad, can you wait for me? I have to speak to Mr. Pearce."

His father looked slightly surprised, but nodded his head. "All right, son. We'll collect the children and wait in the car."

Ben had to wait until the Rev. Pearce had shaken hands and said a few words to every member of his congregation as they left. Then the minister was able to turn to Ben, who looked rather nervous.

"Well now, Ben," he said kindly. "And what can I do for you?"

"Well——" began Ben hesitantly. "I—I think

I want to become a real Christian like my mum and dad."

The minister asked him into the little room behind the church, and they talked together for some fifteen minutes. Looking back, Ben could not remember exactly what he had said, or what Mr. Pearce said, but after they had prayed together he knew that his sins were really forgiven and that he was starting a new kind of life because he had asked the Lord Jesus Christ to give him the eternal life that is promised in the Bible.

He thanked the minister, said goodbye, and ran to join his family in the car. The younger children were becoming restless, and there were sighs of relief as Ben squeezed into the back seat beside his sisters. No-one asked him what had kept him so long, and at first he felt shy of telling. Then he remembered how the minister had impressed upon him the importance of confessing Christ, and when they were half-way home he said suddenly, "Dad, I'm a real Christian now, like you and Mum."

"I'm glad, son," was all that his father said, but in the driving mirror Ben could see that his eyes looked brighter and more twinkling than he had ever seen them. His mother's eyes shone, too, all the lines seemed smoothed from her face, and she hugged Stevie tight as he sat on her lap. Ben felt pleased that he had given them such happiness. It gave him a nice, warm feeling inside.

It was strange, too, how everything outdoors looked fresh and new. Ben had always loved the country, and hoped to be a farmer himself one day, but it seemed that never before had the grass and budding hedges looked so green, the April sky so blue, the clouds so white. It was as if he saw everything through new eyes. Even the sight of a golden cocker spaniel being taken for a walk did not make him feel envious, as normally it would. He felt as though he could never feel bad or unhappy again.

"I didn't know being a Christian could make you feel so good," he said as they went into the house for dinner.

His father smiled and put an arm round his shoulders. "I'm glad you feel that way," he said. "But don't forget, son, that Christians have their trials and troubles the same as anyone else."

Ben could hardly believe him. In his new mood of exaltation he helped his mother finish her preparations for dinner; he helped Stevie, who was having difficulty in mastering his knife and fork; and after the meal he helped his mother to wash up. It seemed that nothing was too much trouble for him in his new-found happiness.

After lunch his father went as usual into the sitting-room and sat down in his armchair. For a while he read from the big Bible, then he just rested. Sunday was the only day that a fire was lit in this room, since it would have proved too expensive to keep both the kitchen and sitting-room fires in fuel every day.

The sitting-room boasted a large sofa and matching armchairs, still new-looking because they had been used so little. There was a square of red-flowered carpet in the middle of the floor, and red curtains at the window. When the curtains were drawn on a winter's evening the room seemed a very cosy place, though not quite so friendly, thought Ben, as the farmhouse kitchen. One always had to be a little careful in the sitting-room. His mother spent a great deal of time on a Saturday, polishing the floor and the furniture, and she didn't like to see finger-marks on the shining wood. There were china ornaments about, too, which could be all too easily knocked over.

Sunday was the only day when Ben saw his father sit down to rest in the afternoon. His mother tried to keep the children quiet on Sunday afternoons. "Let Daddy rest," she would say. "He works so hard all the week that he deserves it."

When the dishes were put away Ben wondered if there was anything he could do to help his father, too. He went into the sitting-room and asked him.

"Well yes, Ben, you could take a look at the ewes and lambs for me, please," said his father, stretching his slippered feet to the blazing logs. "There were no new lambs this morning, but maybe some are coming by now."

Ben went through to the kitchen and put on his wellington boots and his old jacket. On his way out he had to step over old Toby and Floss, who were lying on the doormat. Floss looked up at him with a bright brown eye and thumped her tail, and he paused.

"Come on Floss, Toby—come with me," he said encouragingly, but neither of them moved. They knew that Ben's father was their master and they would go with no-one else. When he came out of the house they would get up and follow him, but until then they would lie and wait.

Although it was now mid-April there was a cold tang to the air. Ben welcomed the freshness of it after the warmth of the farmhouse and walked quickly, hands in pockets and heart still uplifted from the morning's experience. Lambing was in full swing and his father had the in-lamb ewes in the paddock near the house. There were no new lambs, and Ben left the paddock and began climbing towards the hilly field near Dixon's Wood, where the ewes with older lambs were. To Ben's surprise, as he neared the field he noticed that something seemed wrong. The ewes and lambs were clustered together in the corner near the gate, the deep bleats of the ewes and the shrill cries of the lambs mingling in an agitated chorus.

Ben climbed the gate and stood on a top rung, scanning the field and trying to see what the matter was. At first he could not see anything amiss; then, as he watched, a brown-faced ewe detached herself from the flock and trotted, bleating, across the field to the hedgerow nearest Dixon's Wood. She nuzzled something on the ground, and Ben could make out a still, white patch of something near the hedge. It was the brown-faced ewe's lamb and something was obviously the matter with it.

Ben jumped from the gate and ran across the field. As he approached the ewe turned and looked at him with eyes which seemed to plead for help. To his horror, Ben saw bright patches of red against the white of the lamb's still body. He knelt and turned it over, feeling sick. The lamb was dead, covered in blood but still warm and limp. It was badly torn and mutilated and Ben realised with a stab of horror that something—a fox or killer dog—had been at work.

He dropped the lamb and turned and ran towards home. The sun had gone in, and the world, which had been so bright and beautiful a moment before, now seemed a dark and cruel place.

CHAPTER THREE

THE FOX HUNT

"It's foxes all right," said Ben's father, looking serious as he examined the mangled body of the lamb. "Probably a vixen with young ones. They get bold when they're hungry."

Ben was still out of breath from running home to fetch his father and hurrying back to the field with him.

"What will you do?" he panted.

"Nothing, today," said his father, beginning to wrap up the dead lamb in an old sack he had brought with him. "Tomorrow I'll get Bill Martin and Tom and perhaps a few others and we'll track down the foxes and shoot them. When they've killed once they're likely to do it again. No lambs would be safe. I shouldn't really have left these so near the wood."

The dogs sniffed at the sack as he hoisted it onto his shoulder. The mother of the dead lamb bleated pitifully and trotted after them as they set off for home. Ben's heart felt heavy with pity for her. "It seems so cruel—the sheep don't harm anyone," he said sadly.

His father glanced down at him. "That's the way

of nature, son," he said. "The harmless things are often the ones who are preyed upon. There are far fewer meat-eating animals than vegetarians, you see, and those that need meat have to be extra cunning and cruel to get it."

Ben hadn't thought of it that way. He pondered for a while on the balance of nature.

"I suppose God knew what He was doing when He made them like that," he said at last.

"You can be sure He did," said his father decidedly. "God always knows what He is doing."

The lamb was disposed of and the bereaved ewe penned with the other sheep in a safer pasture near the house.

The following afternoon Ben arrived home from school to find a scene of activity around the back door of the farmhouse. Their nearest neighbour, Bill Martin, whose large farm adjoined theirs, was there, together with his cowman, Tom Briggs. They had each brought their dog, and both men carried shotguns and ammunition. The little girls were sitting on the porch steps and staring wide-eyed at the tall men.

"Ah, Ben, my boy," said Bill Martin jovially as Ben approached. "We're going after those foxes. Coming with us? Chris would have come but he had too much homework." Ben hesitated. He did not particularly relish this sort of expedition and shrank from seeing animals hurt or bloodshed of any kind. But he knew that his father also hated killing and only did so when it was absolutely necessary, putting aside his personal feelings. What was good enough for his father was good enough for him, thought Ben.

"Yes, I'll come," he said, making up his mind.

"You must change your clothes and have some tea first," said his mother, coming out from the house. "You can easily catch the men up."

Ben went up to his bedroom and hurriedly changed out of his school clothes. Somehow he felt less hungry than usual and could only eat half his normal amount at tea.

"Are you all right, Ben?" asked his mother. She looked a little anxiously at him, and added, "You don't have to go with them, you know, if you don't want to. No need to make yourself ill."

"I'm not going to be ill," said Ben, though in truth he was already feeling a little squeamish.

"And keep well away from the guns," his mother called as he left by the back door.

The three men and their dogs were already out of sight as Ben crossed the paddock, skirted the Four Oak field which had just been planted, and came to the steep field below Dixon's Wood. He toiled up the slope, passing the place where the lamb had been killed, and climbed the wire fence surrounding the wood.

Dixon's Wood was very large indeed; some people said that it covered a hundred acres. No-one knew how it had come to be called by its name, or who Dixon had been. To Ben it had always been a friendly place where as he grew up he had spent happy times building tree-houses or making dens and caves in the undergrowth. Now it seemed to have a sinister feel, to be a slightly frightening place where killer foxes lurked.

Almost at once he could tell where the others were. The dogs could be heard barking and whining, the men talking excitedly. Ben hurried at once in the direction of their voices, and found them clustered round the roots of a large old oak tree which had been uprooted in a storm. Tom Briggs was already digging under the roots while the four dogs sniffed and whined eagerly.

Ben's father looked up at his approach.

"Are they in there?" asked Ben, eyeing the hole under the roots which was steadily opening up under Tom's shovel.

"Yes," said his father. "There's foxes in there all right—the dogs soon sniffed them out. Probably a nest of young 'uns and we hope the old ones, too. Better to make a clean sweep while we're at it."

"Won't they get out another way?" asked Ben, interested in spite of himself.

"No, lad," said Bill Martin. "Foxes have only one entrance to their hole. We'll get them if they're in there, though they might put up a fight. Here, Tom, let's have a turn."

He took the spade from Tom and began to dig, panting a little because he was quite a fat man.

After a while Ben's father had a turn, then handed the spade back to Tom.

"I think we're nearly there," he said. The dogs

were showing their mounting excitement with little, suppressed whining sounds. Jack Jackson turned to his son.

"Better keep well back, Ben," he warned. "The fur is likely to fly in a minute, and I don't want you in the middle of it."

Ben retreated a little way to the shelter of a nearby tree and watched. The next moment a sudden fury erupted from under the fallen tree roots. A streak of snarling red-brown fur shot from the hole, followed by another slightly smaller. Both launched themselves at the dogs, snarling and snapping like wolves. The dogs were equal to the occasion, however, and for a moment all that could be seen was a seething mass of animated teeth and black, white, brown, and russet fur.

The men stood helplessly by, unable to shoot for fear of hitting their dogs. Then suddenly old Floss gave a sharp yelp and retreated, with blood streaming from a gash in her right shoulder. For a second she stood at the fringe of the melee, then gathered her strength and plunged again into the fray. In that moment, however, Tom Briggs was able to get a clear sight on one of the foxes, and a shot rang out, leaving one of the red-brown bodies limp and lifeless. Ben's father called his dogs, and as they reluctantly drew back the second shot put paid to the other fox.

Ben's heart was pounding as he emerged from his shelter and joined the others. The two foxes lay torn and bloodstained, but still somehow proud and splendid, he thought. Their beautiful fur was soft and thick, russet-brown on the upper parts and white underneath, and their white-tipped tails were long and bushy. He noticed their pointed ears with black backs, and long, sharp, pointed muzzles. Remembering how bravely they had fought for their lives, he felt admiration and pity for the dead wild creatures.

The dogs had had enough excitement for the present and lay panting and licking their wounds. Bill Martin turned over the body of the smaller fox.

"A vixen—and with young cubs, too, by the look of her," he said.

"They'll be still here, then," said Tom, picking up the spade and turning to the hole again. A little more digging revealed the offspring of the dead foxes—three small cubs, blunt-nosed and as pretty as pictures. They were about the size of an ordinary domestic cat. The three of them huddled together, making little whining sounds of bewilderment and fear. Ben's heart went out to them. He thought he had never seen such beautiful little creatures.

'Best get it over with quickly," said Bill Martin, picking up his gun again. "Seems a shame though, doesn't it?"

He fired twice and was about to dispatch the third cub when Ben could suddenly stand it no longer. He ran forward and grabbed their neighbour by the arm.

Bill Martin looked at him in astonishment. "Careful, Ben, careful," he admonished, lowering the gun. "Don't ever do that to anyone with a gun in his hand. What's the matter?"

Ben looked at Bill Martin but addressed his father.

"Oh, please," he said in a choked voice, "Please Dad, don't kill that cub. Please don't."

His father came forward and put his hand on Ben's shoulder. "We've got to, son. Come on now, don't make a fuss. Perhaps you shouldn't have watched us."

Ben shook himself free and ran forward to where the cub cowered beside its dead brothers. He knelt beside it and touched it gently.

"I won't let you—I won't," he said fiercely. The russet fur felt like softest velvet, and beneath the fur he felt the terrified trembling of the little creaure. "You shan't shoot it—you'll have to shoot me first," he said from between clenched teeth.

His father came and crouched beside him, while the others stood by, undecided and surprised.

"Look, Ben," he said reasonably, "if we leave it, this cub will slowly starve to death—a cruel, agonising end. Let us finish it off quickly. It can't live on its own."

"It won't have to—I'll look after it," said Ben. The idea had just leapt into his mind of taking the cub home and looking after it himself. He didn't intend to give it up even for his father.

"I'll look after it," he repeated stubbornly.

Bill Martin shrugged his shoulders helplessly and unloaded his gun.

"He means it, Jack; he'll not give in," he said with a grin. "He's like my lad—got to have his way. Let him keep the cub."

"I knew a chap once who had a pet fox," remarked Tom Briggs. "Real friendly little chap he was, too. I forget what happened to him."

Ben's father rose to his feet with an air of resignation. "Well, I don't know what your mother's going to say, but—all right, you can keep the cub."

Ben felt weak with relief and gratitude. "Thanks, Dad. I'll look after him all by myself. I promise."

"Watch out as you pick him up," advised Tom Briggs. "They've got sharp teeth, even little 'uns, and he might snap."

But the little cub did not snap as Ben slipped his hands under it and lifted it. It merely trembled a little more and cowered against him as he cuddled it against his chest. A musky smell hung about the small animal, but Ben thought he rather liked it. He held it tenderly and felt very protective towards it.

I'll call him Cub, he thought. A nice, simple name, so he'll soon get to know it.

The men began preparing to dispose of the bodies of the other foxes.

"Better take the cub home, Ben," called his father over his shoulder. "Though where you'll put him when you get there I just don't know."

Ben did not know, either. But the thought came to him as he set off through the trees that at last he had a pet—something of his very own.

CHAPTER FOUR

CUB

"You certainly can't keep him in the house," said Ben's mother firmly. It was evening, and the family were gathered round the fire in the big kitchen. The two smaller children had been put to bed, much excited about the cub, and the twins were eating their supper in preparation for following them. Ben's father had Floss in the house for once, and was dressing her cuts and wounds as she lay on a sack in the corner of the room. Ben had brought Cub inside, too, and held him on his lap as he sat beside the fire. It was clear, however, that this state of affairs was not to continue.

"He'll have to go," repeated Ben's mother. "You must find somewhere in one of the buildings to put him."

"But he'll be lonely," protested Ben, cuddling the baby fox, who seemed to be asleep. "He's used to company, you see. He'll miss his family. I thought perhaps he could sleep in my room, because I'm his family now."

His mother put down one of Stevie's socks, which she had been darning, and looked a little more kindly at the cub. He certainly was an appealing little fellow, plump and velvety and innocent-looking as he slept with his white-tipped tail curled about him. Earlier in the evening Ben had tried feeding him with an old bottle of Stevie's filled with milk. But the cub had refused to have anything to do with this strange and unfamiliar object.

"Try him with a bowl on the floor," his father had suggested. So Ben filled a bowl and set the cub on the floor close beside it. Almost at once the little animal's sensitive nose had begun to twitch and soon he had crept closer to the bowl and lowered his muzzle towards the milk. To Ben's delight he began to lap the milk like a kitten and didn't stop until the bowl was empty.

"Hm—a quick learner," commented Ben's father. "Looks like his mother had already begun to wean him. He will probably be ready for solid foods soon."

After the meal Ben had taken his new pet upon his lap, where Cub soon curled into a ball and fell asleep.

Seeing that his mother looked a little more sympathetic, Ben was quick to press home his advantage. "I could have him in a box on the floor—with hay or something in it," he said eagerly. "I needn't have him in bed, if you wouldn't like it."

"I certainly wouldn't like it," exclaimed his mother in horror. "In bed indeed—a smelly creature like that. I suppose a box on the floor would be all right at first. When he's bigger he must go outside."

"Thanks, Mum," said Ben gratefully. "I'll find him a box."

The twins had finished their supper and came to sit on the hearthrug, clamouring to be allowed to hold the cub. Ben handed him down to Anna, taking care not to wake him.

"Be very careful—I don't want him to get frightened," he cautioned.

"And you girls must wash again afterwards or you'll smell dreadfully," said their mother.

The twins wrinkled their noses a little at the strong smell of the little fox, but did not really mind it. Their father had finished attending to Floss and was preparing to take her outside. Ben went along to find a box for Cub's bed, and in the tractor-shed they discovered an old tool box which his father said he could have.

"Do you think he'll live and get tame?" asked Ben as they emptied the box and put its contents on a shelf.

"Well, as he's already eating he stands a good chance," said his father. "Foxes tame quite easily if they're caught young. He'll take a lot of feeding, though, as he grows bigger and needs meat to eat."

"I can hunt rabbits and things for him," said Ben, feeling that nothing would be too much trouble for his very own pet. "And I'll do without milk so that he can have all mine."

"There's no need of that," said his father. "You need your milk. Reckon I can get a drop more from the cows."

They filled the box with soft hay and took it indoors. When Ben went to bed that night he carried the box with him, with the still sleeping cub inside it. He placed it beside the bed, undressed, and knelt beside the bed to say his prayers.

Since the previous day, when he had asked the Lord Jesus into his heart, Ben's prayers had been a great joy to him. He really felt that he could talk to the Lord as a friend, someone who cared about him and all his hopes and plans. It was the same with Bible-reading; now he could see why his parents loved God's Word so much, with its precious promises, guidance and commands. To Ben it suddenly seemed a living Book, through which God could speak.

Tonight Ben felt almost bursting with thankfulness. Everything good seemed to be happening to him all at once. He even had the pet that he had longed for all his life.

As he rose from his knees he looked again at Cub before climbing into bed. The little fox still slept, curled in a ball amongst the hay.

"He's better than any dog," was Ben's last drowsy thought before he fell asleep.

Sometime in the night Ben was awakened by a pattering sound on the floorboards. He sat up and switched on the light. Cub was awake and padding round the room, making anxious little whining noises. His bright eyes and erect ears made him look very wide awake as he blinked at the sudden light. Ben remembered that foxes sleep by day and do their hunting by night.

"You'll have to get used to doing things our way —sleeping at night and being awake by day," he told the little fox, climbing out of bed.

The cub ran away at his approach and hid under the bed. Ben crawled after him and pulled him out. The cub trembled but did not bite or scratch as Ben had feared. But when he was put back into his box he immediately jumped out and began trotting round the room again, sniffing inquisitively at the furniture. He nosed at a low bookshelf and a large book fell to the floor with a crash. Ben feared that he would awaken the children in the next room and arouse his mother's wrath.

"Cub, come here," he said in exasperation, crawling after him again. But the little fox was determined not to stay in his box. Ben caught him for the third time and considered taking him into bed with him. But he remembered what his mother had said and dared not risk it. With a sigh of resignation he pulled the eiderdown from the bed and lay down on the rag rug, holding Cub in his arms. The little fox wriggled and twisted for a while but eventually gave up and fell asleep. Ben did not dare move, and soon he and his pet both slept under the eiderdown.

Ben was stiff and cold when he awoke, and could not at first understand what he was doing on the floor. Then he remembered Cub and looked around for him. To his astonishment the little fox had wriggled out of his arms and was now curled up in his box again, sound asleep. Ben picked him up.

"Oh, you're hopeless," he said in half-laughing exasperation. He washed and dressed and carried his pet and the box to the kitchen. His mother was there, cooking breakfast. She looked askance at the fox in Ben's arms.

"Well, did he behave himself?" she asked.

Ben thought he had better not mention where he had spent the night. Anyway, no harm had been done.

"He wasn't too bad," he said.

Cub was hungry and soon lapped up the milk Ben gave him. A sudden thought struck the boy.

"Mum, whatever shall I do with him while I'm in school?" he asked. "Can he stay in the kitchen?"

"No, he certainly can't,' said his mother emphatically. "He'd be more trouble than an extra child—far more. He can stay in the empty chicken-run while you're away. I'll feed him if you like," she added, relenting a little.

It was surprising how soon Cub seemed to settle down to his new life. By the end of a week he was waiting eagerly for Ben's return from school each afternoon, velvety muzzle pressed against the wire. When another week had passed he knew his name and would run to Ben when it was called. Ben was surprised and delighted when one day the little fox began to trot at his heels like a dog. From then on the two of them became inseparable and were never apart except when Ben was at school. The little fox knew and tolerated the rest of the family, but Ben was the one whom he loved; his own 'family'. At night Cub slept soundly in his box beside Ben's bed; by day he frisked about the large wire chicken-run like a puppy. To everyone's surprise, the two dogs Toby and Floss did not declare war on the baby fox, as had been expected. They did not make friends with him, either, it was true, but as long as Cub kept his distance they were content to put up with him.

To Ben's delight, Cub thrived and grew bigger day by day. Sometimes his parents would look at the fox and wonder what would happen when he became fully grown. But such worries never entered Ben's head. Cub was the friend he had always wanted, and he imagined that they would spend the rest of their lives together.

CHAPTER FIVE

CHRIS MARTIN

"I'm going to Martin's for the tractor and seed-drill," said Ben's father, putting his head into the dairy where Ben had just finished washing the milk buckets. "Want to come?"

"Yes—if I can bring Cub to show Chris," said Ben.

"All right—but you'll have to hold on to him on the way back," said his father.

Ben shut the dairy door and crossed the scullery to look for Cub. He found the little girls and Stevie playing with him outside the back porch, rolling over and over on the flagstones like a nest of puppies. Ben smiled and watched them for a moment. "Cub. Cub," he called softly. "Come on."

The little fox detached himself at once from the group and ran over to Ben, ears erect, eyes bright and questioning.

"Come on," repeated Ben, picking him up. "we're going visiting."

It was early May and outdoors the weather was soft and mild. The starlings above Ben's window chattered and fought in their nest, sending bits of twigs and hay floating down as he passed. They were almost ready to fly, and so big that the nest would hardly hold them. The trees and hedges were covered with a layer of tender green leaves, and the hawthorn tree near the yard gate was a froth of white, sweet-smelling blossom.

"Summer'll be early this year," remarked Mr Jackson as he and Ben set off together down the farm track. "I must get those mangels in while the good weather holds."

Cub frisked at their heels as they turned off the track through the pasture gate and began to cut across the fields towards Bill Martin's farm. On their return journey with the big tractor and drill they would have to take the road, but on foot this way was much quicker. Occasionally Cub would dart off into a clump of bushes as a movement caught his eye, but he always came to Ben's call. Toby and Floss, trotting close to their master, ignored him. They considered him a tiresome puppy, far beneath them socially and hardly worthy of their notice.

After crossing three more fields and skirting a small spinney they turned into the smooth tar-mac'd road which led to Bill Martin's farm. When they had rounded the first bend they were in sight of the farmhouse. This was large and impressive, like everything else about the Martins. The house had a new wing, recently added, and several new and modern farm buildings. A double garage stood beside the house, housing the two cars. There was an air of affluence about the place which always struck Ben in contrast to his own humbler home.

Bill Martin had come from a wealthy family, and this, together with the fact that he was a hard worker and a shrewd business man, had put him in the enviable position of owning the largest and most profitable farm in the district. Ben's father depended upon him for the loan of his up-to-date machinery and equipment, in return for which Jack Jackson worked on the Martin farm at harvest and other busy times. This arrangement suited them both very well, and the two men respected each other and got along well, though Mr. Martin sometimes considered Mr. Jackson a fool about his religious beliefs.

"I see Bill's new milking parlour is finished," said Ben's father, eyeing a long new concrete and steel building to one side of the yard. "I must have a look at it while I'm here."

Already Bill's sheepdogs were heralding their arrival and just then Bill Martin himself appeared at the door of the new building, greeting them cheerfully.

"My, that cub of yours is doing well," he said, looking at the little fox, whom Ben had picked up at sight of the strange dogs.

Ben glowed with pride. "He's tame, too," he said. "He follows me everywhere."

"Chris will be tickled pink to see him," said their neighbour. "You go along to the house, Ben, and find him."

The two men disappeared inside the milking-shed and Ben made for the house, still carrying Cub. As he skirted the farmhouse, heading for the back door, a fair-haired boy a little taller than himself came out to meet him. Chris Martin was a couple of years older than Ben; he had no brothers or sisters, and was rather pampered and spoiled. He attended a private school fifteen miles away and was supposed to be brainy. In spite of this, he and Ben, who hated school, had been on casually friendly terms for many years.

"Hallo," said Chris, his eyes going at once to the pet fox in Ben's arms. "Is that your cub? Isn't he super! Can I hold him, Ben?"

Ben handed Cub over somewhat reluctantly, and Chris began to stroke his russet fur. But the little cub would not settle down. He was nervous with strangers and began to whine and wriggle, trying to get back to Ben. At last Chris had to hand him back, looking a little annoyed.

"I thought he was supposed to be tame," he said disparagingly.

Ben did not like the implied criticism of his pet. "He is tame—" he began to protest, but was interrupted as Chris's mother appeared at the kitchen door.

"Oh, Ben—how nice to see you, dear," she exclaimed. "And is that your dear little pet fox? Do bring him in to show me."

Mrs. Martin was a plump, pink-faced woman who was rather inclined to be gushing. She ushered the boys into her spotless modern kitchen which was equipped with every labour-saving device Ben had ever heard of and several he had not. He perched uncomfortably on the edge of a tubular metal chair, while Mrs. Martin plied him with lemonade and exclaimed over Cub.

"What a dear, sweet little fellow," she said, patting him on the head like a puppy. "And how is your mother, Ben? Busy, I expect, with all those children. I do admire the way she manages all on her own."

In spite of her words Ben felt the note of superiority in her voice.

"She's quite well, thank you," he said politely but stiffly. He drank up his lemonade and stood up. "I'd better see if Dad's ready," he said, and thankfully made his exit. Chris followed.

Their fathers were still inspecting the new milking parlour, and could be heard inside the building discussing its merits.

"Like to see my new bike before you go?" asked Chris.

He usually had some new possession to show off. Without waiting for an answer he ran to the garage and reappeared wheeling a gleaming new sports model. Ben dutifully admired it.

"It's a beauty," he said, and watched as Chris mounted the bike and rode it round the yard, showing off a great deal.

"Want a ride?" he asked, coming to a halt.

"Well—no thanks," said Ben, who was not much interested in things mechanical. "I'd like to see

Judy's puppies though," he added.

"Oh—all right," said Chris, a little huffily. He had expected Ben, who had scarcely anything of his own, to jump at the chance of a ride on the super new bike. They walked in silence to the barn, Ben carrying Cub. Judy, the black labrador bitch, lay in her basket with a mass of shining, squirming coal-black puppies. Ben dropped to his knees beside them, putting Cub down on the floor.

"They're beautiful,' he said, picking up a fat little pup and holding it against his cheek. It smelt sweetly of hay and felt like warm velvet. All the same, he decided, no pup could compare with Cub, who was now frisking about the barn floor and playing with a wisp of hay. Chris watched him thoughtfully.

"Ben," he said suddenly, "I've had an idea. How about selling me Cub?"

Ben look up in astonishment. "Selling Cub? No, I can't. He's not for sale."

Chris kicked at a hay bale. "I'll give you five pounds for him," he offered. "I've never had a fox for a pet, and I'd like one."

"I don't want five pounds," said Ben. "I told you—he's not for sale."

Chris looked sulky, but stubborn. "Well—how much *do* you want, then? Tell you what—I'll swap you one of Judy's puppies for him. They're pedigree and worth a lot of money. Dad won't mind."

Ben put down the wriggling, black puppy and

stood up. He called Cub and picked him up when the little fox came running. Ben hugged him tightly.

"He's not for sale," he repeated. "I won't swap him for a puppy or for all the money in the whole world. He's mine."

Chris had not often been refused anything he wanted, and now grew suddenly furious. He turned away and again kicked viciously at a hay bale.

"Keep your filthy fox, then," he said from between gritted teeth. "I don't want him."

He strode off, letting the barn door bang behind him. Ben stood feeling bewildered and rather hurt. He hugged Cub tighter and whispered, "I wouldn't ever sell you, Cub—not for anything."

He left the barn, fastening the door carefully behind him, and went to wait for his father in the yard.

Soon a tractor engine roared into life, and Bill Martin appeared on the big red machine, with Ben's father following. Mr. Martin halted the tractor and jumped down. "There you are then, Jack," he said. "Hope you can get your roots in before the end of this dry spell."

"Thanks, Bill—I'll bring it back as soon as I can," said Mr. Jackson. "Hallo, Ben," he said, noticing his son. "Didn't you find Chris, then?"

"Yes, I—I think he's gone to the house," said Ben uncomfortably. They bade goodbye to their neighbour and climbed aboard, Ben clutching Cub tightly. They hadn't driven far before Mr. Jackson noticed how silent and preoccupied his son seemed.

"Anything wrong, Ben?" he asked, speaking loudly to be heard above the engine. "Quarrel with Chris or something?"

Ben wondered how his father had guessed. He nodded. "He wanted to buy Cub, and I wouldn't," he muttered.

"What's that?" asked his father. "Speak up a bit. I can't hear you."

"He wanted to buy Cub," repeated Ben, leaning close to his father's ear. "And he didn't like it when I wouldn't sell him."

His father did not answer, and Ben wondered if he understood. "Well, I couldn't, could I, Dad?" he appealed. "Would you, if it was your fox?"

His father turned and glanced at him, and Ben saw a twinkle in his bright blue eyes. Then he shook his head. "No, I wouldn't—and I'm glad you didn't, either," he said. "We'd have come to a pretty pass if we let money count more than a living thing that we're fond of, be it human, dog or fox. 'Course you couldn't sell him, Ben, any more than I could sell one of you children or old Toby or Floss."

Ben was reassured. He knew, however, that the long-standing friendship between himself and Chris Martin would never be quite the same again.

"But I don't need him," he said to himself, looking down at Cub's black-backed, erect ears. "I've got Cub, and he's my best friend—the best friend in the world."

CHAPTER SIX

TROUBLES

"They're coming up nicely," said Mr. Jackson with satisfaction, leaning on the gate looking out across the root field. Ben joined him, with Cub at his heels, and looked at the rows of little green shoots showing against the dark brown soil. It was a fortnight since the mangels had been planted, and during that time they had had some spells of soft, gentle rain, just what the root crops needed to start them into life.

Planning was all finished for this year, and it would be a fortnight or so before the first hay was ready to cut. Next week they would be sheep-shearing, but this week found Ben's father with more spare time than usual on his hands. He and Ben were taking half an hour before tea to inspect the growing crops. They moved on from the root field towards the next one, where the winter corn was growing. Here Ben's father did not look so pleased. He walked in amongst the twelve inch high green spikes with a frown on his face, bending here and there to inspect them closer. Some of the shoots of corn were yellowish and withered-looking.

"What's the matter with it?" asked Ben.

"Wire-worm," grunted his father. "That rain must have brought them out. Still, they've not done much damage yet, and maybe if it keeps dry they won't spread too much."

Ben's stomach was beginning to rumble with hunger. "I think it's tea-time," he said.

His father straightened up with a grin. "Hungry again, are you? You must have hollow legs. Well, come on; we've seen everything now."

They left the field, fastening the gate, and set off for home. The two dogs trotted as usual close to their master's heels, but Cub frisked in front and around them, his russet coat gleaming and his white-tipped brush streaming behind like a banner. He had grown a great deal during the two months that he had lived at the farm, and now had a large appetite. Ben's mother often complained that too much of the family's meat supply went his way.

They reached the house and went into the scullery to wash their hands. The two dogs flopped down onto the mat, but Cub impudently jumped over them and pranced into the house after Ben, who couldn't help laughing at him. His mother, however, was not amused.

'Shut him up in his pen, do, Ben," she said, pouring water into the teapot.

"Oh, Mum, can't he stay in just till after tea?" pleaded Ben. "It's such a nuisance having to shut him up and then go to fetch him afterwards."

"Well—all right," agreed his mother reluctantly. "But leave him in here. I won't have him in the kitchen at meal-times."

Ben shut the door on the cub and went into the kitchen. During tea his mother had more to say on the subject of the little fox.

"I've been changing your bed linen," she said severely to Ben. "And what do I find but nasty, red fox hairs all over the bedclothes. I thought you promised not to take him into your bed with you."

"I know, Mum," said Ben guiltily. "But he will keep getting out of his box and jumping up on the bed. I just can't stop him doing it."

"Well, he's been in your room long enough," said his mother firmly. "It's time he began to sleep in the run, where he belongs. It's plenty warm enough now."

Ben thought it best not to argue any further.

"All right, Mum," he said meekly, and helped himself to another slice of cake.

Suddenly there was a tremendous crash from the scullery. The children squealed and Ben jumped to his feet in alarm.

"That fox," cried his mother. "He's broken something."

She got up and flung open the door, followed by the children and their father. A scene of devastation met their eyes.

Mrs. Jackson had left a large crate of eggs on the table, ready to be collected next day by the egg dealer. Cub had jumped up beside it, and put his paws against the box, pushing off the lid with his nose. It had fallen back on its hinges, and the weight of the lid, combined with that of Cub standing against it on the other side, had overbalanced the box and sent it crashing to the floor. Broken eggshells, yellow yolks and slithery whites lay everywhere, and in the midst of it was Cub, eagerly licking up the mess from the floor and devouring it.

"Oh," said Ben's mother furiously. "Six dozen eggs gone to waste! Take that fox outside, before I get a stick to him."

Ben hurriedly dragged the reluctant Cub away. The fox licked the remaining egg from his whiskers and struggled to get back for more. Ben took him outside and smacked him sharply. It was the first time Cub had been hit and he looked at his master in hurt surprise. Ben knelt and put his arms around him.

"Oh, Cub," he said penitently, "I hate to hit you but you mustn't do bad things, you really mustn't. Now I'll have to shut you up for the rest of the evening and keep you out of Mum's way."

Ben spent the evening clearing up the mess from the scullery floor and scrubbing the stone flags and the egg box. His mother looked stern. She worked hard looking after the hens and collecting, washing and packing the eggs. The loss of a week's output made a large hole in her always slender budget. Ben promised to contribute from his pocket money towards the value of the lost eggs, but he knew it would take a long time to make good the loss.

And worse was to come. When Ben got home from school next day he found that Cub had somehow pushed open the door of his pen and was missing. It was an oppressive, close afternoon and he couldn't really blame the fox for wanting to get out of his confined space, but he knew that Cub must be found at once. He called him repeatedly, but Cub did not appear. In alarm he began to search the barns and outbuildings, but there was no sign of the fox.

Then as he happened to pass one of the henhouses in the orchard he glanced through one of the wire-mesh windows and stopped short in dismay. A familiar russet body was inside, and at Ben's exclamation Cub's pointed nose appeared from one of the nesting-boxes, covered with tell-tale egg yolk.

"Oh, Cub—you little thief," groaned Ben.

He opened the door and grabbed the fox by the scruff of the neck, pulling him away from the nests. No eggs could be seen in any of them. Cub had obviously enjoyed a good meal.

Ben stood still in dismay, wondering what to do. Evidently in knocking over the eggs yesterday Cub had discovered he had a taste for them and would take every opportunity of getting more. He knew his mother would be very, very cross. And yet he could hardly keep a thing like this from her. As he stood undecidedly beside the henhouse he saw his father crossing the yard on his way to the house and ran up to him, carrying Cub.

"Dad," he called. "Dad, wait a minute."

His father turned and waited for him. He could tell by Ben's face that something was the matter. When Ben explained what had happened he looked grave.

"That's bad," he said. "He's got a taste for eggs now, you see, and he'll be after them every chance he gets."

"What shall I do?' asked Ben, feeling worried.

"Make his pen more secure, for a start," said his father. "And only let him out when you can watch him every minute. A collar and lead might be a good thing, too."

"I'll buy him one next time I'm in town," said Ben. He felt sad that Cub's freedom must be further curtailed, but he knew there was no way round it.

'Must I tell Mum?" he asked.

"Yes, you must," said his father. He seemed a little preoccupied and stopped by the back door, looking up at the sky, which was unusually leaden and heavy. Little swirls of dust blew across the yard towards their feet, pursued by an irritable wind. Jack Jackson took off his cap and mopped his sweating forehead.

"I don't like it," he said. "I'm afraid we're in for a storm."

Wanting to get the worst over quickly, Ben confessed about Cub's latest misdeed the minute he got indoors. To his surprise his mother was not as angry as he had expected. "What a nuisance," was all she said. Like her husband, she seemed apprehensive about the weather and kept glancing out of the window. The children were tired and quarrelsome because of the heat, and no-one wanted much tea.

After the meal Ben got a hammer and nails and strengthened the doors of Cub's pen and of the wire-netting run adjoining it. He put the little fox inside, and Cub went at once into the inner enclosure and curled up in the straw. Ben fastened it up securely and straightened up, hot and sticky.

It was already getting dark, long before the usual time. Ben went to bed early, but could not sleep. He turned and tossed restlessly, throwing off the bedclothes one by one until only the thin sheet covered him. Even that felt too hot. In the next bedroom he could hear his parents talking in low, worried tones. Rain, and especially heavy rain, was the very last thing any farmer wanted at this time of the year.

At last Ben sank into a fitful doze, to be awakened almost at once by the first low rumble of thunder. A bright flash of lightning lit the room, to be followed by another, nearer clap of thunder. Ben got up and went to the window, and as he reached it the first drops of rain came splashing and hissing down, few at first but soon becoming a torrent. He closed the window and crouched in a chair beside it, feeling a little awed by the violence and majesty of the storm. It had grown suddenly colder, and he fetched a quilt to wrap around himself. The storm went on and on, but before long Ben had fallen asleep and saw it no more.

When he awoke it was daylight and the rain had stopped. He straightened up, shivering a little, and looked out. The sun was shining weakly from a pale, washed-out sky. The plants and flowers in the front garden looked rain-sodden and battered, and almost all the blooms had been blown from his mother's favourite wallflowers. Ben remembered that it was Saturday and hurriedly threw on his old clothes and went downstairs. His parents were in the kitchen, looking solemn.

"Has much damage been done?" asked Ben.

"Don't know yet," grunted his father. "I'm off up to the fields to see as soon as the milking's done."

"I'll come, too," said Ben, wondering how Cub had fared in the storm. To his relief he found him snug and dry, still curled up in his inner enclosure. He came frisking out when Ben opened the door, bright-eyed and as fresh as a daisy.

'Silly old thing—I bet you never even noticed the storm," Ben told him.

The first field that he and his father visited was the big ten-acre hayfield which had been almost ready for mowing. Now the tall grass was battered and spoiled, flattened so much in some places that it would be impossible to cut it. Jack Jackson said nothing as he looked at it, but Ben could see that the sparkle had gone from his blue eyes. In the root field, things looked even worse. The greater part of the tender green spikes of mangels and swedes had been washed up by the roots in the great furrows the length of the field. Those that remained looked battered and sick.

"It'll all have to be replanted," muttered his father.

Ben knew that root crop seeds were very expensive and his heart sank. The storm had done more damage than he had expected, much more than they could afford. He felt a tinge of bitterness as he wondered how God could allow a thing like this to happen to his hard-working father.

CHAPTER SEVEN

MORE TROUBLES

The Jacksons were sheep-shearing. A week had passed since the night of the fateful storm, and the weather had become warm and dry again. The farmyard was a moving mass of bleating, shorn sheep, strange and vulnerable looking without their thick, woolly coats.

In the barn was a scene of great activity. Bill Martin's powerful shearing machine had been borrowed, together with Tom Briggs, and had been whirring away all the morning. The unshorn sheep and lambs were penned in the inner bay of the barn, and it was Ben's job to catch them one by one as the shearer finished the previous one and turned it outside. His father and Tom Briggs took it in turns to use the shearing machine, while the other rolled up the thick fleeces, tied them with the leg and tail pieces and deposited them in the big wool sack suspended between two beams.

Ben watched his father bending over a ewe and working with long, clean strokes of the sharp cutters. If, as sometimes happened, the cutters nicked the tender skin, it was Ben's job also to fetch the bottle of black oil and dab some on the cut. But Jack Jackson was a careful shearer and did not often need the black oil. The greasy smell of sheep hung over everything, and Ben's hands were greasy, too. He was thankful when he saw his mother coming from the house with a large jug of lemonade. This was the signal for the machine to be switched off and for everyone to have a breather.

Mr. Jackson straightened up and mopped his sweating brow. He took a mug of lemonade from his wife and drank it gratefully, first wiping his hands on a piece of rag.

"Hot work," he commented.

Stevie and Mary had followed their mother from the house, and began clamouring for a ride in the wool sack. Remembering what a treat this had been in his younger days, Ben lifted them in one by one and swung the big sack of fleeces gently. They shrieked with delight, and the grown-ups smiled indulgently at them.

After refreshing himself with a draught of lemonade, Tom Briggs felt in the mood for a little farming gossip.

"Storm do much damage here?" he asked, sitting on one end of the shearing bench.

Ben saw the smile go from his father's face.

"Some," he said briefly, as though not wishing to discuss the subject.

"Flattened our mowing grass proper," went on Tom. "I suppose yours is the same?"

Jack Jackson nodded and rose to his feet, returning his empty mug to his wife. He turned and lifted his two youngest children to the floor.

"Run along with Mummy now," he said. "It's not safe for you here while we're working."

He turned to the shearer and began cleaning the cutters, which had become clogged with grease and wool. Ben knew that he didn't want to talk about the storm and the damage it had done. To a farmer of Bill Martin's standing it would be a nuisance and a loss, but not the major disaster it had meant for the Jacksons. As well as spoiling the hay and root crops, the rain had encouraged the wire-worm in the winter wheat, which now looked yellow and sick all over the field. Mr. Jackson had replanted the mangels and swedes, but there was nothing he could do about the other crops.

"It seems so unfair," Ben had said to his father the day after the storm. "Why does God make things so hard for us, while people like the Martins, who don't care about Him, have it so easy?"

His father had stopped and looked at him seriously.

"Never say anything God does is unfair," he said. "We may not like or understand things that happen, but if we are obeying God we must trust Him to know what is best for us. Even if it means giving up farming."

Ben was horrified when he heard those three words 'giving up farming'. He had not realised that things were as bad as that. He knew instinctively that farming was in his father's blood and his own, that neither could be really happy in another occupation. Yet his father was willing to give it up if the Lord willed it so. Ben wished that he had even a quarter of his father's faith.

The morning wore on, and by midday more of the sheep had been shorn. Tom Briggs would be staying to dinner, and he and Jack Jackson carefully fastened up the barn before going to the house, to stop the unshorn sheep escaping and mixing with their shorn contemporaries. As they went off towards the house, Ben slipped off to the orchard to visit Cub in his run. The young fox was pawing at the wire and whining. He knew that Ben was at home and could not understand why he was still penned up. His new collar and lead hung on a nail beside the pen. At sight of his master Cub began to prance eagerly, his ears pricked and expectant. Ben let him out for a moment to frisk on the grass.

"You'll have to stay in this afternoon," he said regretfully. "The sheep would be frightened if they saw you amongst them—they'd think you were a wild fox."

Cub jumped up with his paws against Ben's legs like a dog, and Ben stroked his thick red fur.

"I'll try to take you for a nice, long walk this evening if we finish early enough," he promised.

It was evening before all the sheep were shorn, and by that time Ben wanted nothing but to scrub himself free of grease and fall into bed. He let Cub out for another short run before feeding him and shutting him up for the night.

"I'm too tired to take you for a walk," he said

wearily. "But tomorrow's Sunday, so I'll get up nice and early and we'll go for a nice, long walk before breakfast."

He went to bed early, tired out, and fell at once into a deep sleep. When he awoke it was early morning and the first sun was streaming in through his window. Ignoring his Sunday clothes laid out over a chair ready for church, Ben slipped into his everyday things and went quietly downstairs. He let himself out by the back door, sniffing the fresh balmy air. Everything had a bright, newly-minted feel about it early in the morning, he thought, making his way to the orchard.

As he approached Cub's pen there was no sign of the young fox in the wire run. He must be asleep in the inner enclosure, thought Ben, though it was odd that he had not heard him and come prancing out as usual. Then as he reached the pen he realised why. Cub was not inside it, and a freshly dug hole, not large, but large enough to take the body of a small fox, showed where he had made his exit.

Ben stared at the hole, neatly burrowed from one side of the wire to the other, in dismay. This was the first time Cub had ever attempted to dig his way to freedom. "It's my fault," said Ben to himself, "for I kept him shut in all day yesterday. He must have been desperate to get out."

He began to search for his pet. The henhouses were all shut up, their occupants sitting on their perches and clucking with surprise as Ben peered in through their wire windows. At least Cub couldn't have disgraced himself by stealing more eggs. But where could he be?

Ben began to search the barn and other buildings, calling, "Cub, Cub", but there was no sign of the young fox. He must have gone off to the fields hunting or something, thought Ben. There seemed nothing to do but to keep searching until he was found. He set off through the paddock and into the near meadow, searching along the hedgerows and calling Cub's name.

One by one he went through the fields until he had covered almost all their land. The sun had risen high in the sky, and an ache in Ben's stomach told him that it was a long way past breakfast time. His family would be wondering where he had gone, and soon it would be time to get ready for the morning service. But he felt he couldn't rest until Cub had been found and brought home. Wearily he trudged across meadows and up banky fields, through the little coppice and along the lower margins of Dixon's Wood. He peered into the leafy depths of the wood, wondering if Cub could have returned to the place of his birth. But somehow he didn't think so. Though born a wild fox, Cub had become so domesticated that he regarded the farm as his home and Ben as his 'family'. Ben didn't think he would stay away willingly for long.

At last, having covered each field of the entire farm, he sat down under a hedge to rest and think out what to do next. It was obvious that Cub had strayed a long way away from home. But he must keep searching until he found him, thought Ben desperately. Cub was not a wild fox, used to hunting for his own food, and he might easily starve if he were not found. The next thing to do, he decided, must be to ask the neighbouring farmers if he could search their fields, too.

Bill Martin's was the nearest, so he would begin there. He jumped up and started across the field to the hedge which divided the Martin farm from their own, and found a convenient hole to squeeze through. He emerged at the top of a steep pasture grazed by some of Bill Martin's sheep, also newly shorn. At the bottom of that field lay another flatter one, and beyond that he could see the long, elegant buildings of the Martin farm.

Perhaps Chris might even help with his search, thought Ben, as he started down the slope, though he didn't really think it very likely. Since Ben's refusal to sell Cub to him, Chris had not been nearly as friendly as before, and a rift had developed between the two boys.

Ben was half-way down the length of the field when he stopped suddenly as a sound came to his ears. He stood still and listened for a moment, holding his breath. There it was again. Above the deep bleats of the ewes and shriller cries of the half-grown lambs was another sound—a faint, whimpering cry of some animal in pain. It could be a dog—or a fox.

"It's Cub!" Ben exclaimed aloud, trying to decide where the sound was coming from. "Cub—Cub—" he called, and listened again. There was another whimper, ending with a yelp of pain, and Ben decided that the sound came from near the hedge on his right. He raced across with fast-beating heart, scattering the sheep, and began to look up and down the hedgerow. At first he could see nothing among the undergrowth and brush which grew thickly at the base of the hedge. Then another whine and a faint rustling in a thick bramble bush sent him racing to the spot. He flung himself down on his knees and began tearing apart the brambles with his hands, never noticing the scratches that soon covered them. Before long the familiar russet face and black-backed ears of Cub were revealed, his eyes dull with pain. He whined frantically as Ben touched him, but did not come leaping out to greet him.

"Poor old Cub," said Ben comfortingly. "All tangled up in the bushes, are you? Never mind; I'll soon have you free."

He redoubled his efforts, breaking off branches of the prickly brambles and pushing them out of the way. Then he gave an exclamation of horror. As he uncovered the rest of the little fox a terrifying sight met his eyes. The supple, russet body was twisted awkwardly, and now he could see why. Cub's right hind leg was a mangled, bloodstained mess, and it was caught tight between the cruel steel jaws of a gin-trap.

CHAPTER EIGHT

CUB'S ACCIDENT

For a moment Ben could only stare in horror, rooted to the spot. Then Cub began to whine again, tugging at the injured leg.

"Easy, Cub, easy," whispered Ben and held him until the fox stopped struggling and became limp in his hands. Only his eyes showed the pain he was in as he looked imploringly up at his master.

"I must get him out," muttered Ben. He felt sick and dizzy, but set to work to clear a space in the undergrowth around the trapped animal. This type of gintrap was released by pressure and he needed room to work. When he had a clear space he bent and took hold of Cub round the body, at the same time putting his foot upon the trap and pressing down as hard as he could. The stiff steel jaws opened a little, but not enough for him to withdraw the mangled leg. He had to release the pressure of his foot and start again, and Cub let out a heart-rending yelp as the cruel trap tightened over his torn flesh once more.

Ben rested for a moment, sick and shaking all over. His strength seemed to have left him and he felt weak and helpless. With an effort he pulled himself together and bent over the cub again. This time he was able to get the jaws open wide enough to allow him to pull Cub's leg away. By this time the young fox was almost mad with pain. He struggled and scratched to get away, his injured leg dangling uselessly from Ben's arms. Ben fought to hold him still, and did not let go even when Cub's sharp teeth sank into his thumb. "Cub, Cub," he sobbed despairingly, "you'll hurt yourself more, you will, you will——'

At last the fox became quieter and drooped dejectedly in Ben's arms. Ben did not try to touch the wounded leg, but he knew from the useless way it dangled that it was broken. His tears gave way to a slow, burning anger against whoever had planted the trap. But his first concern must be to get Cub home and see what could be done for him. Holding his pet carefully against his chest he got up and began to make his way home.

When at last he reached the farm he found only his father there, sitting alone in the kitchen, dressed in his Sunday clothes. He sprang to his feet as Ben came in, and stared at the cub.

"Why, Ben—what's happened?" he asked.

"Cub got out, and he was caught in a trap," said Ben, feeling close to tears again. "Oh, Dad, we've got to help him. Look at his leg—it's awful."

"Now steady—steady," said his father, putting his hand on Ben's shoulder. He went through into the scullery and took a clean towel from the drawer, spreading it on the table.

"Now put him down here and let's have a look at him," he said.

Influenced by his father's calmness, Ben felt suddenly calmer, too. He carried Cub into the scullery and laid him on his side on the towel, holding him down gently. Mr. Jackson touched the wounded leg and began manipulating it gently, talking quietly the way he did when one of the children or an animal was ill.

"Where are Mum and the kids?" asked Ben, suddenly noticing the quietness of the house.

"Gone to church," said his father. "We waited a bit for you, then I told her to drive the little ones in and I'd stay behind and wait for you."

Ben had forgotten that it was Sunday, and he was amazed when he looked at the clock and saw that it was almost twelve.

"Was Mum worried?" he asked.

"She was a bit," admitted his father. "But I told her you must have taken Cub for a walk and forgotten the time." He straightened up and wiped his hands on the edge of the roller towel. Cub lay limp and impassive under Ben's hands, his russet coat stained with darker patches of dried blood.

"What do you think?" asked Ben anxiously.

"Well, it's broken all right," said his father. "I think the best thing would be to wait until your mother comes home with the car; then I'll drive him into Hadley to the vet."

Ben looked at him gratefully. He had been afraid that his father would say that Cub must be put to sleep, as had one of the dogs when it was crushed by a tractor wheel. But perhaps the vet would be able to patch Cub up.

Just then they heard a car pulling into the yard, and saw from the window that it was Mrs. Jackson and the children returned from church. A moment later they came bursting into the room.

"Oh—Ben," said his mother in relief. "Where have you been? I've been that worried. It's not like you to go off like that— Oh!" She had seen Cub's bloodstained body lying on the table, and broke off. Her husband was already herding the younger children into the kitchen in case they should be upset at the sight of the injured animal.

"What has happened?" asked Ben's mother, coming close. "Poor creature—how did he get hurt like this?"

Ben explained about Cub's escape and the trap.

"Poor creature," repeated his mother, touching the russet fur. To Ben's surprise he saw tears in her eyes, and this sign of tenderness towards Cub from his mother made his own eyes suddenly fill with tears. Then his mother became her usual business-like self again.

"Never mind—the vet will soon fix him up," she said cheerfully. "Better wrap him in the towel—you don't want blood all over the car."

On the way into Hadley Ben sat beside his father, holding Cub swathed in the towel. The fox seemed to have lost all fight, and drooped limply across his lap.

"He must have struggled for hours in that trap—worn himself out," said Ben.

"Cruel things; they're illegal now, too," said his father. "I wonder who laid that one, and what for. I didn't think Bill Martin went in for catching rabbits that way. Well, here we are."

They found Mr. Peters, the young vet, at home and he agreed to see them although he was off duty. He was very kind, and the first thing he did was to give Cub a shot of something to relieve the pain. Almost at once the fox was stretched out looking for all the world as though he was dead. But Ben could see his chest rising and falling as he breathed, and knew that he was still alive.

After examining the leg Mr. Peters looked serious and took Ben's father to one side. Ben could see them discussing something, then his father shook his head and he heard Mr. Peters say, "Well, all right then. I'll do my best."

Ben wanted to stay in the room while Mr. Peters set the leg, but his father made him go to the waiting-room. He sat uneasily on the edge of a hard chair and waited there for what seemed a very long time. At last the surgery door opened and his father appeared, carrying Cub's still unconscious body.

For a second Ben's heart stopped beating. "Oh, Dad," he gasped. "Is he dead?"

"No, no," said his father reassuringly. "He's just still doped, that's all. Come and help me get him in the car."

Ben let out his breath in a sigh of relief. He saw that Cub's injured leg was completely encased to the hip joint in a neat plaster cast.

"And will he be all right?" he asked Mr. Peters, who had followed them from the surgery.

"He should be," said the vet kindly. "That leg should knit together and be out of plaster in a few weeks. He'll probably have a limp for the rest of his life, though."

They thanked Mr. Peters and drove off with Cub stretched out on the back seat, his plaster-clad leg sticking out stiffly. Ben sat beside him to make sure he did not get jolted on to the floor.

"Poor Cub," he said, stroking the pointed nose. "He'll have a job to get around at first with his leg like that."

"At least it'll help to keep him out of mischief," commented his father.

By the time they reached home the effect of the anaesthetic was beginning to wear off, and Cub was stirring groggily. Ben carried him into the house and fed him with sips of warm milk. His mother seemed still sympathetic, and he took advantage of her mood to ask if Cub's box could be brought back indoors. He was pleasantly surprised when she agreed.

"But only till he's well again," she warned. "Once that plaster cast's off he'll be into everything again and then out he must go."

Ben put his arms around her middle and gave her a big hug.

"Oh, go on with you," she said, half-laughing as she disentangled herself. "I know you and your cupboard love."

It took a surprisingly short time for Cub to get used to his immobile hind leg. Within a few days he was hopping around on three legs, the plaster cast sticking out stiffly behind. He looked most peculiar, but didn't seem to mind when all the Jacksons laughed. The leg obviously gave him no pain, but Ben sometimes caught Cub looking back over his shoulder at it in surprise, as if he wondered what strange thing was attached to him. He was far less agile than before, and could no longer climb into the henhouse or dig holes, for which Ben was thankful. It gave him a little breathing space, when Cub didn't have to be watched so closely.

A week after Cub's accident Ben's school broke up for the summer holidays. Never very fond of school, he was overjoyed. More than six weeks of glorious freedom! Of course he knew that it wouldn't be all leisure, for he would be expected to help on the farm. But farm work was such a pleasure to him that it hardly seemed like work at all.

The hay had been cut the previous week and was 'making' in the two fields. Much of it, flattened by the storm, had been impossible to cut and was wasted. The rest was poor stuff, wet and heavy, but the Jacksons were making the best of a bad job. Every day they turned the hay, and soon it would be ready for baling with Bill Martin's modern baler.

On the first day of the holidays Ben went to the larger of the two hayfields, armed with a large hay-rake. His father owned an ancient hay turner, with which he worked the main part of the fields, but the hay nearest the hedges had to be turned by hand. Cub hopped along with Ben to the field, almost his old frisky self again, and lay under the hedge while Ben worked.

It was Cub who suddenly gave warning that someone else was in the neighbourhood. He did not bark as a dog would but leapt to his feet and stood stiffly, facing the hedge and making uneasy little whining sounds. Looking up from his work Ben saw that Chris Martin was approaching the gate in the hedge.

"Hallo, Chris," said Ben, preparing to be friendly, though remembering the unpleasant ending to their last meeting. "Hallo," grunted Chris. He climbed the gate and sat on it, glancing at Cub with a look which he intended to be indifferent, but which grew increasingly curious as he noticed the plaster cast.

"What's the matter with his leg?" he asked at last, his curiosity getting the better of him.

"He got it caught in a gin-trap," said Ben, leaning on his rake. "He dug himself out of his run and roamed off and got caught."

"Was his leg broken?" asked Chris with interest.

Ben did not like the almost gloating expression

on the other boy's face. "Yes, it was," he said shortly and turned back to his raking.

Chris remained sitting on the gate and watching him. He had a pocket full of small pebbles and began throwing them idly at dock plants and clumps of grass. Then one flew wide and hit Cub on his good flank, making him yelp sharply.

"Don't do that," said Ben, annoyed. "He's been hurt enough."

"I bet I know where he got caught in the trap," said Chris tantalisingly, swinging his legs.

Ben looked at him. The other boy had a smug, gloating look, and a sudden suspicion flew into Ben's mind. The trap had been laid on the Martin land, and Chris seemed to know something he wasn't telling. Could it have been he who had laid that cruel trap in the hedge?

"I bet I know," repeated Chris.

Sudden anger overwhelmed Ben as he remembered Cub torn and bleeding in the cruel steel jaws. He threw down the rake and went over to the gate. Scarcely knowing what he was doing he reached up and caught Chris by the arms, dragging him from the gate.

"Hey, wait a minute," said the boy indignantly, his fair skin flushing. "What do you think you're doing?"

"It was you, wasn't it?" said Ben from between gritted teeth. "It was you who set that trap."

He swung his fist and hit Chris hard on the jaw,

making him stagger backwards. Chris gasped, then recovered himself and flung himself on Ben, and the next moment the two of them were struggling in a bitter, desperate fight.

CHAPTER NINE

THE FIGHT AND AFTER

It was not long before Ben and Chris had lost their footing and found themselves rolling over and over on the ground, still fighting. They punched and scratched and bit, forgetting all the rules in the heat of the moment. Chris was the older and slightly larger of the two, but Ben was stronger so the two were fairly evenly matched. As they fought, Cub circled round them warily, making anxious little noises in his throat and wondering what was happening.

The ground sloped slightly towards the hedge, and during the winter and spring a small stream trickled through the gully beside it. Even now there were still pools of stagnant water and patches of mud there. As the boys fought they gradually rolled and slipped down the slope, and a last desperate heave brought them slithering into a muddy, nasty-smelling puddle.

The shock of the sudden wetness made them cease struggling for a moment, and this gave Chris a chance to stagger to his feet. He looked a sorry sight, his clothes covered with mud and green slime and torn in several places. His nose was bleeding from one of Ben's punches. He gasped and panted, trying to speak, but no words would come. Then he turned and struggled through a hole in the hedge and went off in the direction of his home, holding a handkerchief to his bleeding nose.

Ben lay in the mud where he had fallen and watched him go. His anger seemed to evaporate as suddenly as it had come, and he felt ashamed of his sudden attack. Indeed, he thought miserably, it had been a most unworthy act from someone who had accepted Jesus Christ as his Saviour and was trying to follow Him.

He dragged himself wearily to his feet, looking ruefully at his soaked and mud-spattered clothes. His boots and socks were soaked through, and there was even mud and slime in his hair. His right eye was beginning to swell, and he touched it tenderly, knowing that it would be black by next morning. Cub came up and licked his muddy knees and Ben picked him up and cuddled him. "Oh, Cub," he sighed dismally, "I do love you, but I seem to be always getting into trouble because of you."

He wondered whether he should go straight home to change or stay and finish turning the hay. Finally deciding on the latter, he found his discarded rake and carried on from where he had precipitately left off. By the time the job was finished he was weary and aching all over, and the mud on his clothes was beginning to dry and harden. He called Cub and set off for home, wondering what he was going to say to his parents.

On reaching home Ben shut Cub up and tried to sneak into the house without attracting attention from his family. But his mother saw him at once.

"Why, Ben Jackson, whatever's happened?" she exclaimed in horror, dropping an empty saucepan with a clang.

"I had a fight," said Ben sheepishly.

The younger children stared at him, agape with astonishment, and he wished he could become invisible.

"A fight, indeed," said his mother. "Come on now; don't sneak off. I want to know all about it."

Ben told her how it had happened, while at the same time she washed the dried mud from his face and applied something cool and soothing to his black eye. Then his father came in for dinner and he had to tell the whole sorry story all over again. When he had finished his father looked grave.

"You did wrong to pick a fight like that," he said quietly, and Ben felt even more ashamed.

"But it was dreadful of Chris to set that trap and then gloat when Cub got caught in it," he protested.

"It's wrong and cruel to put down gin-traps," agreed his father. "But if Chris did do it, it was on his father's land, where Cub had no business to be. You were certainly wrong to hit him, and you'll have to apologise."

"Oh, Dad," protested Ben, but his father would listen to no arguments. "Every Christian should be willing to humble himself and admit when he's wrong," he said. Ben knew that this was true, but it seemed hard to have to apologise to Chris. All the same, he knew he must do it.

"I'll go this afternoon," he said.

"But not before you've had a bath and made yourself respectable," added his mother. "You look like a walking scarecrow."

After dinner Ben got out the old tin bathtub and filled it with hot water. The Jacksons had often talked of installing a modern bathroom, but there was never enough for a luxury of this kind. Every penny of profit seemed to be swallowed up by the farm. He knew his mother dreamed of having a real bathroom with hot and cold running water, and his father had promised to have one put in as soon as he could afford it. In the meantime the family managed as best they could with the old tin tub in the scullery.

Ben discarded his muddy clothes and scrubbed himself clean, washing his hair and cleaning his dirty nails. When he was clean he rubbed himself dry, put on a clean shirt and jeans and emptied the bath down the sink. He was just finding a dry towel for his hair when he was surprised to hear a knock at the front door. This was unusual, for most callers to the Jackson farm came to the back door. Ben heard his mother answer the door and the sound of voices, then the sound of the closing of the sitting-room door. Next moment his mother came hurrying out into the scullery, looking puzzled.

"Mr. Martin wants to see your dad," she said to

Ben. "He says it's not on business, so I've put him in the sitting-room. Go and fetch Dad from the machinery shed, will you?"

With the towel still over his head Ben ran to the shed where his father was fixing something on the hay turner. He came at once, wiping his hands on a piece of rag, and went straight into the parlour.

As Ben sat in the kitchen rubbing his hair dry he could hear the deep voices of the two men rising and falling, but he could not tell what they were saying. Once or twice Bill Martin's voice seemed to rise angrily, and Ben and his mother looked anxiously at each other. It seemed an age before they heard the door opening and their visitor being shown out. A moment later Mr. Jackson came into the kitchen, his face more drawn and worried than they had ever seen it. He slumped down in his arm-chair, and Ben's mother went to him in alarm.

"What's the matter, Jack?" she asked, putting her hand on his shoulder.

Her husband seemed about to speak, then looked across at Ben. "You go outside for a while, son," he said.

Ben guessed that they wanted to speak privately about something Bill Martin had said. He also guessed that it concerned himself and the fight he had had with Chris.

"Can't I stay, Dad?" he asked. "If it's to do with me, then I'd like to hear."

'Well, I suppose you may as well," said his father wearily.

"Was it about Ben fighting young Chris?" asked his mother.

"Well, partly that, yes," said his father. "It seems that Chris went home in a dreadful state this morning, crying and covered with blood and saying that Ben had attacked him for no apparent reason."

"But there was a reason," cried Ben. "That trap——"

"Yes, the trap," interrupted his father. "Bill mentioned that. It seems that Chris had nothing at all to do with it. It was set by an old tramp who was round here months ago. Tom Briggs surprised him one morning laying a similar trap, and the fellow cleared off in a hurry and must have left the other one behind."

Ben's heart sank like a stone. So his attack on Chris Martin had been completely unjustified!

"But Bill Martin is a reasonable man," protested his mother. "He knows that boys fight and things like that."

"I'm afraid he's not so reasonable when it comes to his son," said Mr. Jackson heavily. "That boy is the apple of his eye, you know, and Bill is taking this very seriously. In fact, the outcome of it is that he's decided to put an end to our working arrangement."

Ben and his mother stared at him in horror.

'You mean you won't be working for him any more, and he won't be lending us machinery?" asked Ben at last.

"That's right," said his father. "He says he wants

nothing more to do with us."

"Oh, Jack," said Mrs. Jackson in dismay.

Ben was silent, horrified and dismayed by this last bitter blow to his father. Without the use of Bill Martin's modern equipment they would be virtually unable to get on with the farm work. And it was all due to his own nasty temper. How he wished he could undo the events of the morning!

"Perhaps when I've been to apologise he'll change his mind," he ventured timidly, but his father shook his head. "I'm afraid no amount of apologies will change Bill Martin's mind once it's made up," he said.

"But what will we do?" asked Mrs. Jackson anxiously. "We have no money to buy our own machinery."

Her husband shrugged his shoulders resignedly.

"We'll just have to face every job as it comes and do it as best we can," he said. "That's all we can do, apart from praying."

"I'll help all I can, Dad," said Ben eagerly, anxious to make amends. "I can do as much as a man, and we'll get the work done between us."

His father smiled sadly at him but said nothing. He got up from his chair and went out, his shoulders more bowed than Ben had ever seen them. The children's voices floated in through the open window as they laughed and played in the yard. Ben looked at his mother and saw how strained and worried she looked. He knew without telling that a very hard time lay before all of them.

CHAPTER TEN

STILL MORE TROUBLES

The alarm clock shrilled its long, harsh note and Ben rolled over to switch it off, reluctant to face another hard-working day. But he knew he must get up, and threw back the covers, yawning and still half asleep. He washed quickly and flung on his working clothes, then knelt beside the bed for his morning prayers.

Somehow prayer was not the joy it had been when he had first started his new kind of life with the Lord Jesus. Often his mind seemed full of other things—Cub, or farm work, or the troubles they were having. He knew that sometimes these things came first with him, and that this was wrong. But there seemed to be nothing he could do about it.

He sighed and rose to his feet, stretching to try to ease the stiffness in his back and arms. They had finished hay harvest, laboriously piling the hay in cocks and hauling it in loose instead of in the usual bales.

Now it was August and they were ready to begin cutting corn. There was no question of borrowing Bill Martin's combine harvester, so Ben's father had got out the old binder and managed to get it into working order. How they would thresh the corn later they did not know. They would worry about that when the time came. All this time Ben worked with his father from dawn to dusk, six days a week. Never in his life had he worked so hard. By the end of the day he was so exhausted that it was often as much as he could do to crawl into bed. There was no time for playing games or fishing or exploring or doing any of the things he usually did in the summer. There was no time even for playing with Cub.

At the thought of Cub, Ben hurried downstairs and out into the orchard to feed his pet and let him out for a short run. The plaster was off his leg now, and he could run as well as ever, though with a slight limp. But Ben knew that he fretted and pined at being shut up all day, and his coat was growing dull from lack of exercise. Sometimes he sulked and would not come out from his sleeping place.

"He's sulking this morning," Ben said aloud as he approached the pen and saw that it was empty. Then his eye fell on a neat hole burrowed under the wire, and his heart sank. Cub had rediscovered his digging abilities and had escaped during the night. Ben put down the food, too discouraged even to search for his pet. At breakfast he told his parents of Cub's escape.

"He'll be okay; he's plenty big enough to look after himself now," his father said reassuringly. "He'll be back before long, you'll see."

His mother sniffed. "It'd be a good thing if he never did come back, if you ask me," she said. "That animal's been nothing but trouble ever since he came here."

"He hasn't," said Ben stoutly. "And I bet he'll come back to me."

All the morning they worked hard, Ben's father driving the tractor and binder while Ben picked up the sheaves and propped them together in stooks. By dinner time his hands were blistered and his back ached from bending. But as they came into the yard all these troubles were forgotten as a red furry streak came rushing from near the back porch and flung itself upon Ben.

"Cub," he said joyfully, hugging the fox. "You've come back. I knew you would."

Cub was now almost too heavy to be carried. He pranced round and round Ben's feet as they walked to the house, his lame leg, newly released from its plaster, looking thin and peculiar. He seemed very pleased with himself and Ben wondered what he had been up to.

"At least he can't have been stealing eggs again," he said to his father. "He's much too big to squeeze in through their hole now."

"Talking of holes," said his father, "you'd better set to and fill up that hole in his run, young Ben. That cub's getting too clever by half."

"He *is* awfully clever," said Ben proudly. But all the same he got the spade at once and went to repair the damage.

Next morning, however, another neat hole had been dug and Cub was again missing. As before, he turned up during the morning, smug and self-satisfied. This happened the next day and the next, and Ben was in despair. He strengthened the sides of the run with pieces of board and buried wire netting below the ground surface, but to no avail. Cub just burrowed deeper and escaped once again.

"I think you're wasting your time trying to keep him in," said his father when this had been going on for a week. "Better just put him out at night and let him run free."

Ben sighed. "I suppose so. But I hope he doesn't go near any more traps." He also had another secret fear—that Cub would return to the woods and forget about him. But so far this hadn't happened. Cub always turned up on the doorstep to meet him, and was content to be shut up for most of the day when his nights were free. His coat lost its dullness and took on a glossy sheen, and he seemed to grow even faster than before. By early September he was almost fully grown.

It was nearly time for Ben to return to school, and still there was almost half the corn to be harvested. He and his father redoubled their efforts. Sometimes his mother brought all the children out to the fields and helped, too. On the very last day of the holidays they brought a big basket of tea things to the field, together with a kettle and the little primus stove.

"I thought we'd have a picnic, as it's your last day," Mother said. "You children haven't really had much fun this summer."

The little ones were thrilled. Having a picnic tea in the cornfield was a real adventure. They ran about excitedly, never minding when their bare legs were scratched by the stubble. The twins helped their mother to set out the food, while their father started the primus and Ben filled the kettle from the nearby spring. The dogs and Cub had come to the field, too, and lay under the hedge looking expectantly at the picnic basket.

Ben was returning from the spring, slowly and carefully so as not to spill any water, when he saw someone walking across the stubble from the field gate. He recognised a neighbouring farmer, Fred Banks, whose land joined theirs and Bill Martin's. He knew Mr. Banks as an easy-going man and was surprised to see as he got closer that he seemed angry. By the time Ben himself reached his parents, Fred Banks was talking to them heatedly, gesturing and waving his arms.

"But are you sure?" Ben's father was asking as Ben carefully set down the kettle.

"Sure enough—I could tell by the limp," said their neighbour grimly. "There can't be two foxes in this district with a limp in the right hind leg."

Ben realised that they were discussing Cub.

"What's wrong?" he asked anxiously, looking from his father to their neighbour.

"That fox of yours has been after my chickens,

that's what's wrong," said Fred Banks, turning to face him. "He got one night before last, so last night I waited up for him. He'd dug a hole under the hen-run as crafty as you like, and got another before I knew about it. I just saw him running off with it—took a shot at him, too, but I missed. It was that fox, sure as eggs."

He waved his stick angrily towards Cub, who still lay dozing under the hedge.

Ben went pale with horror. He didn't know what to say. His father was speaking.

"I'll pay for the chickens, of course, and I'll see it doesn't happen again," he said quietly.

The man seemed slightly appeased. "I know you're straight, Jack, and don't mean any harm," he said. "But it ain't natural, having a tame fox about the place. The thing ought to be shot."

He waved his stick again threateningly, at Cub and then turned and stumped off. Ben and his parents looked at each other, and even the children were silent. His mother was the first to speak.

"Well," she said, stooping to put the kettle on the stove. "We'd better get on or we'll have no tea today."

She began clattering the cups and saucers and putting out more food. But somehow the air of festivity had gone from the picnic.

Ben went close to his father. "I'm sorry, Dad," he began timidly. "I—I didn't think he'd kill chickens. I'll see he doesn't do it again."

His father turned towards him and Ben had

never seen such a stern look on his face.

"You'd better," he said quietly. "We can't keep an animal that's a danger to other people's property. If Cub kills again, then Fred Banks is right—he must be shot."

Ben could not reply. He knew that his father meant what he said. But he also knew that he would never, never let Cub be destroyed. He turned away and went to sit beside the young fox, putting his arm round him protectively. "They'd have to shoot me first," he muttered under his breath.

That night Cub slept securely locked in a large chicken coop which happened to be temporarily unoccupied. It was not nearly big enough for an almost fully-grown fox, of course, and it was plain that he resented being confined in such a cramped space. But it had to do until some alternative arrangements could be made. Cub's nights of roaming the countryside in freedom were over.

The following day Ben returned to school and his mother agreed to keep an extra sharp eye on the fox. But by day Cub was as good as gold and seemed content to romp in the yard or sleep by the back porch whenever he was let out. Ben breathed a sight of relief when he got home and saw him waiting at the gate.

"If you'd only behave at night as well as in the daytime no-one would bother about you," he told him.

Ben's father had managed to get hold of some

timber cheaply from a builder he knew, and planned to build a large, secure shed where Cub would be safe. But until then he must spend his nights in the chicken coop. Already he was reluctant to enter it, and Ben had to drag him the last few yards and bundle him in forcibly when bedtime came. As he walked away he could hear the young fox whining and clawing at the wooden walls. He wished that he could make him understand that soon he would have better quarters.

That night Ben was awakened suddenly by a sound from outside. He looked at his alarm clock and noticed that it was half past three. The sound came again, not loud, but distinct in the stillness—a crunching, ripping sound like splintering wood.

Cub, thought Ben in alarm. He's trying to break out. He threw back the covers and leapt from the bed, not stopping to put on anything over his pyjamas. In his bare feet he ran downstairs, unbolted the back door and made for the orchard. By the light of an almost full moon he could see that his fears were justified. Even as he ran towards the coop he saw a small hole appear with a sound of tearing wood, and a familiar pointed nose appear through it. The next moment Cub was squeezing his long, lithe body through the small space he had made, and was springing to the ground.

"Cub," called Ben sternly. "Come here at once."

Cub came up and pranced around his master, pleased with himself and excited to be free, and Ben made a grab at him. But the fox evidently had no intention of being caught and returned to the hated coop. He avoided Ben's hands, and, with a last playful snap at his bare ankles, turned and streaked away across the orchard.

"Cub, come back," called Ben desperately. But Cub was already at the hedge, and as Ben watched he squeezed through a gap underneath it and disappeared.

CHAPTER ELEVEN

THE RUNAWAYS

It was no use going after Cub. Already he was probably far away across the fields in search of his night adventures, and would not be back until morning. Ben walked disconsolately back to the house, noticing for the first time the roughness of the yard under his bare feet. He let himself in and climbed back into bed, shivering and anxious. What would happen if Cub again visited someone's farm and got into their poultry run? He hardly dared to think about it. For hours he tossed and turned, unable to sleep, and at last fell into a doze just as dawn was breaking.

When Ben awoke he had an ominous feeling of trouble brewing. He had overslept and hadn't much time to get dressed and ready for school. At breakfast he said nothing about Cub, and fortunately his parents did not ask. No-one seemed to have noticed the tell-tale hole in the side of the chicken coop. Perhaps if Cub returned safely without doing further damage they just might get away with it.

Ben spent an anxious day at school, and was twice ticked off by his teachers for not paying attention. On his return that afternoon he felt a surge of relief as he saw Cub's russet body come gambolling to meet him across the yard.

"You're a bad fox," he said sternly, refusing to play with him. "But thank goodness you've come back."

But his relief was short-lived. In the kitchen his father and mother were waiting for him, both with set, worried faces. Looking from one to the other of them Ben knew that something very serious had happened. His father came at once to the point.

"Ben," he said, "did you know that Cub had got out again last night?"

"Well—yes," faltered Ben. "He tore a hole in the side of the coop. I tried to stop him, but he wouldn't take any notice and ran off."

His parents looked at each other. "Has—has he killed another chicken?" asked Ben fearfully.

"Worse than that," said his father. "Bill Martin has been here. He says that last night Cub broke into their turkey-house and butchered about a dozen of the young turkeys they were fattening for Christmas."

Ben felt the colour drain from his face. He opened his mouth to speak but no sound would come. Then he found his voice with a rush.

"It mightn't have been Cub," he burst out. "Why should he want to kill all those turkeys? He couldn't want to eat them all. Perhaps something else did it."

His father shook his head. "No, Bill Martin

heard the commotion and came out. He saw Cub quite clearly. That's the way foxes often are, son; they kill just for the sake of killing. Bill said there were bodies and blood and feathers everywhere."

Ben felt sick. He knew that this time there would be no reprieve for his pet. His mother came over and put her arm round his shoulders.

"We're sorry, Ben," she said. "We know how you feel about Cub. We——" she broke off and looked appealingly at her husband "Jack, couldn't we——"

"No," interrupted Ben's father sternly. "I'm sorry too, believe me, but it's no good. He has to go. We've tried just about every way to keep him for you, Ben, but that fox has meant nothing but trouble. We can't keep him any longer."

Ben turned away, his eyes blinded by sudden tears. His mother moved to follow him, but her husband held her back. "Let him go," he said. "You can say goodbye to Cub, Ben, then I'll get it over with."

Ben stumbled outside, his body racked with sobs. Cub was waiting patiently by the back door, and sprang joyfully at him, expecting a game. Ben took his warm body in his arms and sat down on the step, burying his face in the velvety russet fur.

"I can't let them do it—I can't," he wept silently over and over again. It seemed as though the world had come to an end. Without Cub life would be empty. Then suddenly a desperate plan began to form itself in his mind. "I won't let them do it," he said and stood up, putting the fox from him.

When he returned to the kitchen he saw at once that his father had taken down his shotgun and laid it across the sideboard. At the sight of it Ben's eyes filled with tears again and his mother came up quickly and put her arms around him.

"Get it over quickly, Jack," she begged her husband.

Ben pulled himself free.

"Dad," he said with a gulp. "Couldn't you leave it till the morning? Let me have one more night with him, please."

His father hesitated. "Well——" he began, but Ben interrupted. "He could sleep in my room again—just for this last time, couldn't he, Mum? He couldn't hurt anything there."

"Couldn't we let him, Jack?" asked his mother, and to his great relief his father nodded.

"All right, then; but just this one night." He picked up his gun and replaced it in its usual position on the wall.

"Now come and have your tea, Ben," said his mother.

But Ben couldn't eat. He was not at all clear about what he intended to do, but one thing was certain—he was going to save Cub if he could. In the meantime he must keep his parents from suspecting anything.

He went to bed at the usual time, taking Cub with him. He remembered the first night Cub had come to the farm, and his determination to save him deepened. He got into bed and waited, with Cub on the bedside rug, pretending to be asleep when his parents looked in on him on their way to bed. He lay still for another hour or so in the darkness until he guessed they must be asleep.

Cub was dozing on the floor, but woke up as Ben climbed out of bed. Ben tried to keep him still while he dressed quietly. The moon came out from behind a cloud and shone into the room, and Ben's eye fell on the pile of camping equipment stacked in a corner of the room, untouched since his birthday. He gathered it up and rolled it up as small as he could, taking his rucksack, quilted sleeping-bag and groundsheet. Then he put on an extra sweater and his waterproof anorak and slung the camping gear over his shoulders. All this time Cub sat watching him, his eyes bright and inquisitive in the moonlight.

Ben picked up the fox, who was very heavy now, and tiptoed with him to the door. He paused on his way down the passage as he passed the door of the two younger children, which they always kept a little open at night. The moon shone full into the room, lighting up Mary's long fair hair spread out on the pillow. Stevie was curled up in a corner of his cot, his thumb comfortingly in his mouth. Ben felt a pang as he realised that it might be a long, long time before he saw them again; perhaps never.

For a moment he felt tempted to return to the security of his room and his warm bed. Then he remembered the fate which hung over Cub and hastened on, avoiding the floorboard which creaked near his parents' door. A faint snore sounded from within and again his heart smote him as he imagined how sad they would be to find him gone. But holding Cub tightly he crept downstairs and into the kitchen. There he put down the fox and searched in the larder for some provisions. He found some tins of meat and fruit, and a loaf of bread, which he bundled in his rucksack together with a tin-opener, a plastic beaker and a tin plate.

He hesitated for a while, wondering what else he would need. His eye fell on his little pocket Testament, lying where he had left it after last reading it with his family, and he picked it up, putting it into the pocket of his anorak. He found his torch, and put that in the other pocket. Then he thought he should write a note to his parents. He found a pencil and a scrap of paper and wrote by the moonlit window:

Dear Mum and Dad,

I have taken Cub away. I expect I shall get a job where I can look after him. Don't worry about me.

Your loving son, Ben.

He added a line of kisses, one for each member of the family, and propped the note against the teapot where his mother would be sure to notice it.

There seemed nothing left to do. He put on his wellington boots, picked up Cub again, and let himself out by the back door, closing it softly behind him.

Outside he put down the fox and shivered a little. The warm summer nights were beginning to give way to cooler autumn ones, and at any time now the first early touch of frost might appear. The yard was silent and silvery in the moonlight as Ben shouldered his load and walked across it, followed by Cub. He crossed the paddock and the adjoining field, pausing at the top of it for a last look at the farm buildings huddled below. Then he climbed the gate into the field where he had found the dead lamb, and plodded laboriously up it, feeling the weight of the camping gear heavy on his back.

The dark mass of Dixon's Wood loomed ahead, and he felt a little tremor of fear as he realised that he had never before entered it at night. But it seemed the only place that offered a safe haven for himself and Cub. Reaching the wire fence which surrounded it, he called the fox and lifted him over it, then swung himself over, and together they entered the darkness of the wood.

CHAPTER TWELVE

IN DIXON'S WOOD

Once amongst the trees it was much darker than in the open. The moonlight penetrated only here and there and Ben was glad of the narrow beam of light from his torch. He pushed on between the bushes, his heart thumping a little faster, and Cub followed, sticking close at his heels.

Ben had never before been in the wood at night. All around he could hear strange little rustlings and scurryings in the undergrowth as the small night creatures went about their business. An owl hooted somewhere far away, and was answered by one close at hand, which made Ben jump in alarm. On and on he plodded, his burden getting heavier and heavier on his back. Soon he had left the fringes of the wood and was pushing through unfamiliar undergrowth, as he went deeper into the heart of the wood. Once he stopped and sat on a fallen tree-trunk to rest, then got up and pressed on again, determined to put as much space as possible between himself and the farm by the morning.

Ben knew that his parents would search for him when they found he was missing. A rough plan had formed itself in his mind, by which he intended to hide deep in the heart of Dixon's Wood, camping out and waiting for the hue and cry to die down. Then he would make his way to some far-off part of the country and get a job to support himself and Cub. Perhaps he would even stow away on a ship and go to a foreign country. That a twelve-year-old boy and a young fox would be oddly conspicuous did not even enter his head.

The wood grew denser as Ben and Cub penetrated deeper. The trees seemed larger and closer together and the bushes thicker. On and on he plodded, getting more and more tired and wondering when it would be safe to stop. The moon went in behind a cloud and he began to stumble in the darkness as his weariness grew. At last, after what seemed like hours, he felt compelled to stop.

He had been following a stream for some time and thought that its banks would be a good place to camp. He chose a dry space under a large oak tree and thankfully unstrapped his load. It was too dark to erect the tent, so, feeling exhausted and depressed, Ben laid out the groundsheet, unrolled his sleeping-bag and crept inside it, taking off only his boots. Cub snuggled in and curled up beside him, and Ben hugged him, glad of his warmth. For a few moments he lay listening to the murmur of the stream and the strange whisperings of the trees; then, worn out by his long walk and the happenings of the day, he fell into a deep sleep.

When Ben awoke it was broad daylight and the

sun was high in the sky. He had no way of telling the time but guessed it must be about noon. Cub was still curled up, a tight, warm ball against him in the sleeping-bag. Ben's mood of depression had vanished and he crawled out of the sleeping-bag, feeling light-hearted and adventurous. Cub awoke and stretched himself and bounded to his feet, ready for anything the day might bring.

"Come on, Cub," said Ben cheerfully. "Let's go to the stream and get a drink."

He put on his boots and they raced the few yards to the little stream fringed with ferns. He knelt and drank deeply from his cupped hands, then splashed the clear, cold water over his face. Cub lapped beside him. Ben felt suddenly ravenous.

"Let's get some breakfast," he said.

He went back to his small pile of possessions under the oak tree and began to open a tin of meat. He found the loaf and cut some large hunks off it with the knife the twins had given him for his birthday, which now seemed a very long time ago. At the thought of his family, Ben sobered a little. By now they would have discovered his absence and the note. Sharing his breakfast with Cub, he planned his best course of action for the day.

He decided that he could camp for at least one more night here beside the stream. He knew he was deep in the heart of the wood and thought that it would be safe. Tomorrow he would move to a different spot in case the woods were searched.

"We'll get the tent put up first," he said when

they had finished eating. "You stay by me, Cub—don't go wandering off on your own."

The fox seemed quite content to frolic in the grass and undergrowth which bordered the clearing as Ben began to erect the tent. He had never put up a tent before, and at first the ropes, pegs and poles seemed a hopeless jumble. Then he discovered an illustrated leaflet with instructions and step-by-step diagrams, which simplified matters a great deal. Before long the tent was up, its green canvas blending nicely with the green of the leaves and grass of the clearing. Ben laid out the groundsheet and sleeping-bag inside, together with his rucksack and a few provisions. He had taken off his anorak and sweater as he worked, and piled these in, too.

"There," he said with satisfaction; "that's our home now, Cub."

The afternoon was fine and warm, the sun coming through the trees in little dapples on the grass. A good day for getting on with the corn harvest, thought Ben with a twinge of conscience. He knew that his father would sadly miss his help. But there seemed nothing that could be done about it.

He called Cub and decided to explore this part of the wood. Perhaps they could find some blackberries or early nuts to eke out their meagre supplies. With Cub at his heels he began to follow the stream as it wound out of sight between the trees. But after a while he came to the conclusion that there wasn't much to see. The trees grew thickly all around, with here and there a hollow log where one had fallen. Apart from an occasional rabbit and a few birds, there was no wild-life to be seen.

He found a few blackberries and ate them, but they were red and unripe and had an acid taste. The only nuts on the hazels were immature and soft inside, no good for eating. Feeling hungry again, Ben retraced his steps and followed the stream until they reached camp again. The day was beginning to draw to a close and was getting chilly. Ben put on his extra sweater and began to prepare supper. He cut hunks from the loaf again and opened another tin of meat and one of fruit. Cub was hungry, too, and ate most of the meat.

"We'll have to go easy on the food," said Ben, looking at the few supplies they had left. Even as he spoke Cub made a sudden grab at the remains of the loaf, and before Ben could stop him he had wolfed it down.

"That's all our bread gone," said Ben in dismay.

He wished he could make a fire to sit by, but decided that it would be too risky. Someone might see smoke rising from the wood and decide to investigate. Besides, he had no matches or any means of lighting a fire. It was growing colder and twilight was falling fast. There seemed nothing to do but go to bed. Ben buried the tins under a tree, had a drink of water and crawled into the tent.

"Come on, Cub," he called. "Bed time."

But Cub was not so keen to retire for the night. He would have preferred to have a game in the twilight or to go for a prowl in the wood. He came to the doorway of the tent and peeped in at Ben, then turned and pranced off across the clearing.

"Cub, come *here*," called Ben in exasperation.

Cub wouldn't come. In the end Ben had to catch him and drag him into the tent, fastening the door flap securely behind him. Even then Cub would not settle down but nosed round and round the tent trying to find a way out. It was quite dark before at last he gave up and came to lie down beside Ben in the sleeping-bag. It was a long time before Ben fell asleep. He watched the moon rise and shed silvery bars through the openings of the door flaps. Cub's body felt reassuringly warm beside him, and at last Ben, too, was asleep.

He was awakened suddenly while it was still night. For a moment he lay wondering what had roused him. Then the sound came again—a shrill, barking cry from somewhere far-off in the wood. It came again, and he realised suddenly that it was a fox calling. Cub had heard it, too, and Ben felt him stiffen and wriggle free of the sleeping-bag, listening.

"It's all right, Cub," said Ben, putting out his hand reassuringly. "Just a wild fox. Lie down."

But Cub would not lie down. Next time the cry sounded he made a little whimpering sound and dashed to the door of the tent. Before Ben could prevent him he had torn at the fastenings until they gave way, sprang through the space and was gone into the night.

Ben crawled to the floor and looked out. Cub had run across the moonlit clearing and disappeared between the trees in the direction of the foxes' cries. It was no use trying to look for him. He crawled back into his sleeping-bag, feeling worried and wondering what would happen when Cub met his wild relatives. Perhaps they would attack him and tear him to pieces. Or perhaps he would want to stay with them for good. Ben dozed, waking with an anxious start at every rustle or sound from outside. Towards dawn he was fully awakened when a furry shape came bouncing into the tent and flopped down beside him, panting. It was Cub returned safely.

Ben looked at him in the cold grey light of dawn. The young fox seemed happy and pleased with himself.

"Did you find your wild relations?" Ben asked, putting his arm round him. "I'd like to know where they are and how you got on with them."

Cub licked his face and then curled up to go to sleep. Tired from the long hours of waiting, Ben lay down and soon he, too, slept.

CHAPTER THIRTEEN

THE SEARCHERS

When Ben awoke he found he had again slept late. Again the day was fine, with the sun climbing high in the sky. He and Cub scrambled out of the tent, washed in the cool water of the stream and breakfasted on the meagre remains of their supplies.

"We must get more food today, somehow," said Ben, looking at the one small tin of fruit which remained. "And we're moving to a different camp this morning, too. We'd better get busy."

Cub was still hungry. He nosed around the rucksack, looking for something more to eat.

"It's no good—there's nothing else," Ben told him. "You'll have to catch a rabbit or something."

He wondered if he could train Cub to catch rabbits and bring them back to him. That way they could live in the woods for a long time. But then he remembered that they had no way of lighting a fire for cooking, and regretfully he abandoned the idea. He got to his feet and set about breaking camp and preparing to move on.

First of all he rolled up the groundsheet and sleeping-bag and packed the smaller items away in the rucksack. Piling all these together in a heap he began to dismantle the tent, pulling out the pegs one by one.

He was removing the last one when he suddenly became aware that Cub was behaving strangely. The young fox was running to and fro at the edge of the clearing, peering through the trees in the direction of Ben's home and making anxious little whimpering noises.

"What is it, Cub? What's the matter?" asked Ben, pausing.

He listened for a moment but could hear nothing. But Cub was getting more and more agitated. Ben could see that the hairs on the back of his neck were standing stiffly, as he had seen dogs' do when they were alarmed. Suddenly Ben felt anxious, too. He listened again, holding his breath, and from somewhere far-off in the wood came the faint sounds of voices—men's voices. There was something else, too—the deep woof of a dog.

His heart began to hammer against his ribs in panic. Could the men and dogs be searching for him? There was no time to lose. He must get away from here as quickly as he could. But which way should he go? The dogs might be tracker dogs and would follow his trail whichever way he went. Then he remembered something he had once read—that dogs cannot follow a trail through water. Ben ran to the stream and waded quickly into it, splashing upstream as quickly as he could. Cub ran along the bank beside him, looking at his master in puzzlement. The sound of the voices was getting nearer. Glancing over his shoulder, Ben redoubled his efforts, glad that the trees grew so thickly. He waded along desperately, the water at times trickling inside his wellington boots and soaking his feet. Soon he was out of sight of the camp, and the stream was leading him into a part of the wood where he had never been. The sound of voices grew fainter, but he dared not stop. They must have reached his camp by now, and would know he was in the wood.

At last, gasping and soaked to the knees, Ben paused to get his breath. Cub paused, too, and looked at him enquiringly from the bank. The voices had died away in the distance. He looked around, wondering if there was somewhere he could lie up and hide for a while. The bushes were thick and concealing, but if the dogs came this way they would be able to trace his scent. Then he noticed a large wych-elm tree a little way upstream, whose branches dipped almost to the water. If he could manage to climb the tree straight from the water he would leave no tell-tale scent on land.

He splashed towards the tree and reached up for the stoutest branch he could see. Grasping it firmly he lifted his feet from the water, kicking wildly as he tried to swing his legs towards the trunk. The branch bowed low over the water, but did not break; and after threshing wildly in mid-air for a while, Ben got his legs near enough to grip round the thicker part of it. After that it was an easy matter to work his way along the branch until he reached the tree. He rested for a moment, gasping with his exertions, and taking stock of the situation.

The branches of the tree grew thickly all around the top of the trunk, where he was sitting. The leaves were still thick and green upon it, and Ben was fairly sure he could not be seen from the ground. Then he heard whining from below and remembered Cub. Peering down, he saw that the young fox had crossed the stream and was standing with his forelegs against the trunk, staring up into the branches in bewilderment. Ben wondered if he should climb down and bring him up into the tree beside him. But he knew it would be difficult to keep Cub quiet and still, especially if the searchers came that way. He would almost certainly give them both away. He leaned down and parted the branches to speak to Cub.

"Cub—go away," he said urgently. "Go on—into the wood and hide yourself. *Go away.*"

Cub could not understand. He whimpered at Ben and tried to jump up to join him in the branches.

"Please, Cub," pleaded Ben desperately. "We'll both get caught. *Go away*, please."

But Cub wouldn't go. He began to run round and round the trunk of the tree, whining with agitation.

Ben broke off a twig and threw it at him, hitting him on the flank. Cub stopped with a start and looked at him reproachfully. In desperation Ben broke off a larger branch and threw it as hard as he could. This time it hit Cub hard on the nose, making him yelp with pain. Ben threw another and another, until at last the fox got the message and ran off, disappearing into the bushes at the edge of the stream. Ben breathed a sigh of relief. If only Cub had the sense to stay away!

The sun was at its highest and beat down strongly into the branches. Ben made himself as comfortable as he could, but soon he became unbearably hot. He took off his wet socks and boots and watched them steaming as they dried in the hot sun. Except for the birdsong and the gurgling of the stream there was no sound in the wood. He wondered if the searchers could have possibly given up and gone home. Wedging himself more securely in the tree he dozed for a while in the warmth of the sun. Suddenly he became fully awake as again the sound of voices came to his ears. It sounded as though the searchers were coming his way. He pulled on his half-dried socks and wellingtons and tensed himself, waiting. If only Cub had the sense to stay out of sight!

The voices got nearer, and now Ben could hear twigs snapping as they were stepped on, and the occasional woof of a dog. He sat tight, hardly daring to breath. Soon the men were near enough for him to hear snatches of their conversation. From their few brief remarks he was able to gather that they were indeed searching for him. Cautiously Ben parted the leaves just enough to allow himself to peep through. He saw four large, purposeful-looking, uniformed policemen, two of them with large Alsatian dogs on leashes. The men were carefully and painstakingly investigating every bush and every inch of ground on the other side of the stream. After a moment Ben let the leaves fall gently back into place again, hoping that the slight movement would not be noticed. But men and dogs were intent on their task and did not glance up. They were moving slowly upstream, and Ben let out his breath in a sigh of relief as their voices began to grow fainter and fainter and finally died away in the distance.

But he knew they would be back. He did not dare to climb down from the tree. Shifting his cramped limbs a little he settled down to wait, if necessary until it was dark. The afternoon wore slowly on, and the sun went in. It suddenly grew colder, and Ben shivered as a sudden chilly little breeze rustled the leaves. Then a faint drizzle of rain began to fall. He was protected by the thick, leafy branches, but in spite of these his clothes and hair were soon damp. In the afternoon the men and dogs reappeared, this time searching the wood on his side of the stream. Ben crouched motionless as they passed within a few feet of his tree. Then the danger was past and they were moving away downstream.

Ben stayed in the tree until it was quite dark and he was sure that the searchers had left the wood. It was still drizzling as he climbed painfully to the ground and stretched his cramped, stiff limbs. He felt damp and shivery and his feet were stone cold. He waded across the stream and began to make his way towards his camp, wondering where Cub had spent the day. His feet warmed a little as he walked, but he felt miserable and anxious. He had eaten nothing since his scanty breakfast, and his stomach felt empty and uncomfortable. He thought longingly of the warm security of the kitchen at home, with its cheerful fire and the table laid for supper.

When Ben reached the clearing a further shock awaited him. In the light of the hazy moon he could see that it was bare—the tent, sleeping-bag, rucksack, had gone! He realised at once that the policemen must have discovered the camp and removed all his possessions. Ben could have cried with desolation. Then a faint movement under the tree caught his eye, and next moment the familiar shape of Cub came bounding across the clearing to dance around his legs. Ben knelt and put his arms around him, feeling slightly comforted. At least he still had Cub.

He began to search around for somewhere to spend the night. In the morning they must leave the wood and find somewhere else to stay. At the edge of the clearing was a large, hollow log. Ben crawled inside it and lay down, pulling the hood of his anorak up over his head. Cub crept in beside him and lay down, too. It was very uncomfortable but at least they were out of the rain. Pillowing his head on his arm, Ben hugged Cub and tried to sleep.

CHAPTER FOURTEEN

THE RETURN OF THE PRODIGAL

It was impossible to sleep inside the hollow log, as Ben very soon discovered. There was no way he could get comfortable on the hard, knotty surface, with only his anorak to cover him. Soon he was shivering miserably, his head and stomach ached and his feet felt like lead. Cub was restless and would not keep still, but kept going to the end of the log and peering out. Then suddenly came the high, shrill barking sounds they had heard the night before—the calls of the wild foxes. At once Ben knew that this was what Cub had been waiting for. The young fox sprang to the end of the log and made as though to jump out. Then he hesitated and returned to Ben, pushing his keen, cold nose against the boy's cheek. The thought suddenly came into Ben's mind that Cub was saying goodbye to him. He flung his arms round his pet's neck, burying his face in the velvety fur. Then Cub was gone, streaking away to join his newfound friends.

Ben lay alone and shivering, hoping at first that Cub would return as he had done the previous night. But the long night hours passed, until at last dawn began to streak the sky, and he knew that Cub would not come back. He had returned to the wood where he had been born, and from now on would be a wild fox among other wild foxes.

A sudden great loneliness and despair overwhelmed Ben, and burying his head in his arms he sobbed and sobbed. Now that Cub was gone he was quite alone in the world. He could not possibly return to his parents after the dreadful thing he had done by running away from them. He had no-one to turn to. What was to become of him?

Ben sobbed until he was exhausted, then lay still for a few minutes, aching from head to foot. In spite of his misery he was still hungry. Dragging himself to the end of the log he emerged into the cold grey dawn and sat on the log to search his anorak pockets for some stray crumb that might be hidden there. He found no food, but in the right pocket his hand closed over the little New Testament he had put there when he left home. He pulled it out and looked at it in a mixture of surprise and shame, remembering that he had neither read God's word nor prayed since he had run away. Suddenly he wanted to come to God in prayer, but surely it was no use now? God could never forgive one who had been as bad as he had.

He leafed listlessly through the pages of the little book, and came to a halt at St. Luke's Gospel chapter fifteen. Almost without realising it he began to read at the top of the page. Then suddenly he realised that he was reading the parable of the

Prodigal Son, and that the son seemed remarkably like himself in some ways. He read on, fascinated, wondering what happened in the end. A couple of verses seemed to leap out of the page at him: 'And he arose, and came to his father ... And the son said unto him, Father, I have sinned against heaven, and in thy sight, and am no more worthy to be called thy son. But the father said to his servants, Bring forth the best robe, and put it on him; and put a ring on his hand, and shoes on his feet ... For this my son was dead, and is alive again; he was lost, and is found.'

Ben closed the Testament and put it back into his pocket. He knew that God had spoken to him, and what he must do. He knelt down on the damp grass and prayed simply, "Dear Lord, I'm sorry that I've been so bad. I'm sorry that I've put Cub and myself first all this time, even before Yourself. Please forgive me and help Mum and Dad to forgive me, and help me to truly follow You from now on. Amen."

As he rose from his knees he felt that already a great load had rolled away from his heart. The sun was coming up and beginning to shine in weak rays through the trees. Ben gathered together the last weary remnants of his strength and began the long walk home.

A lump gathered in his throat when at last he emerged from Dixon's Wood and looked down at the roofs of the group of buildings that was his home. It seemed a very long time since he had left it, and yet it had been only two days ago. He climbed the fence and began to hurry down the steep field towards the farm.

As Ben entered the yard his first thought was of surprise that everything seemed so much the same. The starlings could still be heard quarrelling in the eaves, and the two dogs were lying on the mat outside the back door. They looked up as Ben opened the gate, wagged their tails briefly in recognition and settled down again to wait for their master. As Ben approached the back door it opened and the tall figure of a man stood there. At first Ben did not recognise his father. Mr. Jackson looked suddenly old, he walked with a stoop and his movements were slow with fatigue. He did not immediately see Ben, who felt suddenly shy. Then his father's blue eyes fell upon him and a look of joy came over his tired, haggard face. He held his arms wide and Ben ran into them, his shyness forgotten. How comforting was the earthy, familiar smell of his father's old working jacket! For a moment each of them could only clutch the other blindly, unable to speak.

"Son—you're back," said his father at last in a voice gruff with thankfulness.

Ben nodded. "I'm sorry, Dad," he got out, drawing back a little.

"The cub?" asked his father.

"He—he went back to the wild foxes," said Ben with difficulty.

His father nodded. "Better so," was all he said.

Ben realised that he was not going to ask for any more explanations. Some day he would tell his father everything, when it didn't hurt quite so much.

"Go in to your mother," said his father, turning him towards the house. "I'm going to start work."

Ben went slowly into the scullery and through into the kitchen. His mother was there, sitting huddled beside the stove. Her face, too, was haggard, her hair uncombed, her overall creased. It struck Ben suddenly that his parents had not been to bed since his disappearance, and he felt a fresh pang of shame. His mother did not look up as he came in.

"I've put the milking buckets ready, Jack," she said in a weary voice.

"Mum—it's me," said Ben humbly.

His mother came to life and was beside him immediately, holding him by the arms and examining his dirty, tear-streaked face. She said nothing, but suddenly clutched Ben as his father had done. When she let him go he saw tears on her cheeks, but her mouth had its old cheerful smile.

"What a mess you're in," she said, and Ben grinned suddenly at her familiar scolding tone. "There's hot water in the kettle—have a good wash. And when did you last eat?"

"Yesterday morning," said Ben after some thought, and his mother began bustling round preparing breakfast for him.

It was bliss to soak his aching limbs in a tub of

hot water in the scullery, although Ben almost fell asleep while doing so. Afterwards he sat before a huge meal in the kitchen, but found he could scarcely touch it.

"Off to bed with you, then," said his mother briskly. "You look as though you haven't slept for a week."

In his bedroom Ben undressed and sank gratefully into his clean, warm bed.

When he awoke it was evening and dusk was beginning to fall. Ben got up and dressed in clean clothes, suddenly ravenous again. When he went downstairs all his family were in the kitchen at supper. The children fell silent as he entered, staring at him round-eyed and curious as though he were a stranger. His mother turned from the stove. Her hair was now neatly combed and she had put on a clean flowered overall. His father's eyes were bright blue and sparkling as he looked up from his meal.

"Here's your supper, Ben," said his mother, putting a steaming plate of beef stew in front of him. Ben attacked it hungrily. But after eating a few mouthfuls his eye fell on the empty tool box which used to be Cub's bed, lying in a corner of the room. A lump rose in his throat and he was suddenly unable to eat more. His parents noticed his look, and glanced at each other.

"Bill Martin came over while you were asleep," said his mother. "He and all the other neighbours are so pleased that you're home, Ben."

Ben nodded dumbly, his eyes misted with tears. It was good to be home, but how was he going to exist without Cub?

"And our working arrangement is on again," said his father. "He and Tom Briggs are coming to help us finish the corn tomorrow."

Ben nodded again. He was glad about that. His mother had gone to the scullery and came back carrying something in her arms.

"He brought this for you, from Chris," she said gently. "Everyone is sorry about Cub, you see."

Ben looked at what she held. It was a plump, wriggling, half-grown labrador puppy, black and velvety soft.

"One of Judy's puppies," explained his father.

"I don't want it," said Ben gruffly. He looked away. How could they expect him to forget Cub, just like that?

His mother put down the puppy and it began playing on the floor, pouncing on people's feet and pretending to bite them. Mary and Stevie squealed with delight.

Ben watched the puppy's antics out of the corner of his eye, pushing the food around on his plate. The puppy jumped up and put its forelegs on his lap. It nuzzled his hand with a moist nose and bit gently at his fingers. He pushed it away. It was too soon—the puppy reminded him too much of Cub.

But a name for it—Jet—suddenly sprang into

his mind. The puppy jumped up again, and he offered it a piece of bread from beside his plate. Across the table, his mother and father looked at each other and smiled.